Masters of the Heart

*A Modern Spiritual Seeker
Dialogues with the
Great Sages of History*

by
Andrew Canale

PAULIST PRESS
New York / Ramsey / Toronto

Library of Congress
Catalog Card Number: 78-58953

ISBN: 0-8091-0271-4

Published by Paulist Press
Editorial Office: 1865 Broadway, New York, N.Y. 10023
Business Office: 545 Island Road, Ramsey, N.J. 07446

Printed and bound in the
United States of America

ACKNOWLEDGEMENTS

Grateful acknowledgement is herein made to the publishers indicated for their kind permission to quote from the following works:

From *Rolling Thunder*, by Douglas Boyd. Copyright © 1974 by Robert Briggs Associates. Reprinted by permission of Random House, Inc.

Excerpts, abridged and adapted from pp. 27, 52, 53-54, 59, 110, 114, 123, 139, 180-181, 195-198, 200-202, *(passim)* from *Physics and Philosophy* by Werner Heisenberg. Copyright © 1958 by Werner Heisenberg. Reprinted by permission of Harper & Row, Publishers, Inc.

Morton T. Kelsey, *Encounter with God*. Reprinted by permission. Published and copyright, 1972, Bethany Fellowship, Inc., Minneapolis, Minnesota.

Reprinted by permission of William Morrow & Co., Inc. from *The Universe and Doctor Einstein* by Lincoln Barnett. Copyright © 1948 by Harper and Bros. Copyright 1948 by Lincoln Barnett. Revised Edition copyright 1950. Second Revised Edition copyright 1957 by Lincoln Barnett.

T. S. Kuhn, *The Structure of Scientific Revolutions*. Foundations of the Unity of Science, Vol. II, Number 2. Reprinted by permission. Published and copyright 1962, 1970, The University of Chicago Press, Chicago, Illinois.

From *Hosteen Klah: Navaho Medicine Man and Sand Painter* by Franc Johnson Newcomb. Copyright 1964 by the University of Oklahoma Press.

The Collected Works of C. G. Jung, Vol 6: *Psychological Types*, trans. R. F. C. Hull and H. G. Baynes; ed. H. Read, M. Fordham, G. Adler, W. McGuire. Bollingen Series XX. © 1971 by Princeton University Press. Selections reprinted by permission.

Mircea Eliade, *Shamanism: Archaic Techniques of Ecstasy*, trans. Willard R. Trask. Bollingen Series LXXVI. © 1964 by Bollingen Foundation. Selections reprinted by permission of Princeton University Press, Publisher of the Bollingen Series.

Excerpts from "The Journey of the Magi," "Burnt Norton," and "The Dry Salvages" by T.S. Eliot are reprinted from his volume *Collected Poems 1909-1962* by permission of Harcourt Brace Jovanovich, Inc.; copyright, 1936, by Harcourt Brace Jovanovich, Inc.; copyright 1943, 1964, by T. S. Eliot; copyright 1971 by Esme Valerie Eliot.

From *Lame Deer: Seeker of Visions*. Copyright © 1972 by John Fire/Lame Deer and Richard Erdoes. Reprinted by permission of Simon & Schuster, Inc.

From *Black Elk Speaks* by John G. Neihardt. University of Nebraska Press, Lincoln, Nebraska, copyright 1961. Reprinted with permission of the John G. Neihardt Trust.

Sigmund Freud, *The Future of an Illusion*. Doubleday, New York, Copyright 1964. Reprinted with permission of W. W. Norton & Company, Inc.

AUTHOR'S NOTE

I wish to express my gratitude to Richard Payne, Senior Editor at Paulist Press who invited me to write this book. I also wish to thank Professor Morton T. Kelsey of the University of Notre Dame for his consistent support before, during and after the writing of the book. Finally, thanks to my wife, Kay, for her patience, support, loving criticism and proofreading.

Contents

To
Morton Kelsey,
my friend and teacher

Introduction

'A cold coming we had of it,
Just the worst time of the year
For a journey, and such a long journey:
The ways deep and the weather sharp,
The very dead of winter.'
        T. S. Eliot "Journey of the Magi"

Sometimes, even in the cold, we hear the calling, some hidden voice behind the blustery winds. We try not to pay attention to it, to deny that it is even there. No, just some trick played by the wind and trees, magical words trying to crack our shells. If we ignore it, it will pass and go to haunt other ears.

But it remains. After the wind, before the next, in our still quiet pocket, it remains, demanding. "Out into the cold," it says. "There is something to find, something important." We wait; it will stop; it always stops. And comes again.

Why go out there? Others have marked the way, have mapped the territory. We might get lost, in this snow. The markers are covered now, hiding. Why should *we* risk ourselves? What is the reason for this journey?

"It is a word journey, a journey to the Word," that voice answers.

Ah! But he told us already, voice. "Words strain, crack and sometimes break, under the burden, Under the tension, slip, slide, perish, Decay with imprecision, will not stay in place, will not stay still." (Eliot, "Burnt Norton") And you expect us to go on a journey, in the snow, for this?

"Yes."

1

But why?

"You are too comfortable here. Smell the death in this cabin."

Don't we know what we need to know already? Haven't others already shown the way? There is science and religion, Cain and Abel, which are the different ways. Take one, take the other.

"Take both—together."

Ha! That is impossible. They don't fit together, they *can't*, impossible.

"As you said 'Words . . . decay with imprecision, will not stay in place.' "

We don't know what we'll find out there.

"Or in here," answers the voice.

You expect us to go out there alone, in the cold?

"Not alone. Take your tools. Gather together what you know of science and of God and go."

The presence of the voice fades and the howling wind returns. Suddenly the cabin is utterly empty and terribly lonely. It would be nice to see some others though we don't expect any solutions to this word problem. Just in case we'll bring along our tools, for we aren't sure where our journey will take us.

Now we're outside, plodding through high snow and soon we have lost our way. We hold tightly to our tools. As we climb down the great hill on which the cabin sits, we see in front of us new territory. We don't know what we'll find on our word-journey, our science-religion-journey. What was it Rebbe Nahman said to us, before we stopped at the cabin? Oh yes. "Whenever a man interrupts his journey, the roads go into mourning." And Einstein. "Science without religion is lame, religion without science is blind." We had forgotten. There's much that we've forgotten but we've now begun again.

PART ONE

Chapter 1   *At the Bottom of the Mountain*

Trudging through the snow is hard work. At one point, we slip on a hidden rock and slightly twist an ankle. On several other occasions, our weight is too much for the snow base and we find ourselves thigh deep in the white stuff. Meanwhile, body heat melts the snow on our pants making the descent an altogether unpleasant venture.

Gradually as we descend, it becomes warmer and after a whole day's walk it is very warm indeed. It's startling to see how high up we had been. The cabin set in the mountains borders an immense desert. But heavy jackets are of no use

4

down here; ours goes into the backpack. We now remember
why we had stopped there. It had been a very hard climb from
the other direction and we were exhausted. Finding a well
stocked cabin was a touch of luck and we decided to remain for
it was very comfortable. But the comfort made us forget that
we had set out long ago knowing of both the mountain and the
desert. They hadn't frightened us then for we were sure that
we would easily conquer them. The journey, however,
proved more than the thought. Arriving at the cabin after that
long, grueling climb signalled the end. Yes, we'd gone far

5

enough, had discovered enough to satisfy that testy voice.

What! Oh yes, the voice. It had spoken before. How curious! It was the voice which had told us to leave that first time too. We had listened, foolishly as it now seems, and because of it had climbed a huge mountain only to find this desert on the other side. Now the scorching heat burns away all remnants of the voice and but for ourselves, the sun and the sand, all things seem delusions. It was nothing more than a ghastly joke which sent us on our way.

It gets even hotter as the day wears on. Our loneliness brings frightful doubts to travel with us. How are we to survive in this huge desert? When will our water run out? How nice it would be to have a truckload of that snow right now. Whoever is in charge lacks a sense of balance for certainly the moisture would serve a better purpose out here.

Mustn't drink too much water. It will only make us sweat, use all our energy. But what difference? A moment's pleasure, a moment's saturation. There, the water is gone. But horror quickly fills the canteen. We are thirstier than ever, in anticipation, but the deed is done. We trudge on.

The desert air shimmers, for us an enormous radiator. We remember the comforts of the city. Houses, paved roads, trees, a chair. Especially that, a chair under a tree with a glass of lemonade nearby. But was that real, did it ever happen? Or is it just the conjurings of a scorched brain? Or worst of all, is it true and gone forever?

The silence opens an inner desert as immense as the outer one. Used to be that we could easily change the imagery of this inner desert, furnish it, cover it and deny it. Not so right now. That sun is too bright, too powerful, too much in control. We are caught between two worlds which are the same, dust onto dust. We merely serve as a filter between the two. Swallowing outer sand, spewing forth inner sand. Ech! A ridiculous hopelessness captures us and tears would well up if only there were moisture. We try to swallow, kuk, kuk, but the mechanism refuses to work. Smart body. What sense in

6

replacing sand with sand?

The day burns on, the sun now behind us pushing us. Our long shadow slinks before us, evergrowing, promising to become the night. In this strange world it takes on a life of its own, mesmerizing us. Memories of a different time, impossible memories for this little filter, appear before us, within us. Is there a distinction? The land is rolling, dripping, breathing, surreal. Forms appear and disappear. A large grizzly bear (in the desert?) stands before us, menacing, as though forbidding our journey, trying to hurl us back to the mountain. The bear is a good argument for its position but strangely some atavism not mutated away, a power, surges in us and standing on our hind legs we growl back at the bear who steps aside and smiles at us! We pass. In this strange place, we experience many things, some which slip away, unknown as yet but not less real for that. We move among a herd of bison, our thundering hooves a song. Snakes, we slither along the ground. It looks different from this angle with these eyes. We meet a young man along the way and we are forced to wrestle all night with him and like Jacob we limp away wounded in the thigh. We laugh and dance and rejoice until suddenly we remember that we don't understand. The landscape is dripping paint, behind an enormous pterodactyl whose call is the only sound we hear and we run away trying to hide but each sanctuary dissolves, leaving us exposed. Someone rubs our neck, soothing us with some unknown protective chant. Our mind rushes to put it all together while waiting for another dream or vision. This soothing, too, will soon dissolve.

But it doesn't. Instead the fingers solidify the world, rubbing reality into our sore stiff neck, clearing our eyes, relaxing us. We are in a natural shelter, protected by a huge rock from the sun. There are two trees and even some green shrubs just in front of us.

"Tell us what you are doing out here," says a husky voice with a Mideastern accent behind us.

Turning, we expect to see a laughing coyote, or a dinosaur.

But there stands an old man, a man of the desert, who quite possibly spontaneously generated from the sands. Behind him, a young woman with veiled face, looks on waiting patiently.

"Who are you?" we ask.

"First things first. You must tell us what you're doing in the desert," says the old man.

We struggle to remember. "Oh yes, yes. We set out looking for some answers. We'd hoped to find some explanations for our life which had gotten awfully foolish and meaningless."

"Then what, God be praised, are you doing here alone?"

"No one told us how to go, where to go, what to expect. They weren't willing to tell us or perhaps they didn't even know. Only a nagging inner voice kept after us and we knew no other way to quiet it. Whenever we'd get comfortable there it would be again repeating itself."

"And what would it say?"

"That we were on a word-journey, a journey to the Word."

"Obviously a Christian voice. Were there no Christians where you were?"

"None who could answer or even stop the nagging voice."

"But why, God's light never fail us, would you even wish to silence that voice?"

"We get tired of being asked the same questions over and over. This is why we set out on this journey, in hopes of finding an answer."

"Then it is fortunate that we discovered you for we can help you with these questions."

"You can? And who are you?"

"I am called by many names. You shall call me Moses."

"You mean . . .?"

He taps the huge rock once and a stream of water comes from it. Taking the canteen, he fills it and the stream ceases.

"You didn't hit it twice."

"I learned my lesson, God is good, I know who I must trust. But enough of that. You shall know the woman as Ruth. She

8

will join us though you shall not speak to her."

"And why is that?"

"Ah! How quickly you recover your strength! There is a moment for every meeting. You will get to know her another time. Now let us eat; then we shall discuss which way you shall go."

From a pouch he takes some fruit, cuts each fruit into quarters, gives one part to each of us and puts the fourth into a hole in the sand. After sharing four pieces of fruit this way, he closes his pouch. We are amazed at how satisfied this meal leaves us.

"But why did you bury the fourth part each time?"

"Must not the desert eat? How else will it nourish us as we go?"

"You are going with us then?" we ask.

"We will show you the best way to go. The rest is your own journey."

"Let's get going then."

"Not so fast. Before, this attitude was appropriate for it sent you to the desert. Now that you are here there are many choices. You must choose one."

"What choices?"

"In this, your particular desert, they are Indian choices."

"We're to become Indians?"

"You will *meet* Indians if you so desire and learn from them."

"Let's begin."

"God is patient! You forget too quickly your lonely journey. You must be prepared with some notion of what to expect."

"At least tell us the options."

"God pushes you forward! So be it. There are these three choices at this place in the desert. First, there are the Indians who have come to the white man's way. They observe white man's rules and live in small houses doing menial jobs."

"This is just what we have left. They have no more answers

than we do."

"Then there is don Juan, the best known modern Indian, who will show you how to become a warrior, a man of knowledge. Through his apprentice, many searchers have found their way to his truths."

"Tell us more about him."

"He showed Castaneda, his apprentice, that one's perception of the world is only a construction, an explanation, about which one cannot be certain. This construction, which he calls the tonal, is the social person. There is another world, the nagual, that which is mysterious, terrifying and full of wonders, which emerges only through jolts. To establish oneself in this world, to survive in it, one needs allies, which are protectors in the nagual that channel power. According to don Juan, power is the center of the world and does what it wants. At the same time, one can enter a relationship with power, God is merciful, which allows one to balance the terror and the beauty."

"But what is this nagual, how does one experience it?"

"You experienced it before we met."

"And that is all there is?"

"That and one's relationship to it. Don Juan told Castaneda that nothing mattered for him, that all one could hope to do is to witness the nagual for it is the most important part of life."

"Then there is no meaning?"

"One prepares himself for his last dance with death. Death must be one's best friend throughout one's life so that his last dance will be glorious."

"How did Castaneda react to all this?"

"First of all, he hadn't experienced the nagual so don Juan showed him the way into it through psychotropic agents. Don Juan says that only through trickery can one become a man of knowledge. Castaneda then felt a paradox because his construction of reality didn't match his new experiences of reality and so he entered an impasse until he was able to let go of his old construction. When he could do this, he would become a man of knowledge who could witness the nagual, balance the terror and beauty and prepare himself for his last dance with death."

"It's all a preparation for the last dance then?"

"According to don Juan it is, although he allows that, though he finds no meaning, everything might be meaningful for someone else. It's an important position, by the way, because it is a different answer to the destruction of Indian life than those Indians give who incorporate themselves in the white world."

"It still doesn't answer our questions of meaning, our word-journey questions."

"For many others, it answers these questions. It at least allows, God be made known, one to witness the nagual, to acknowledge the existence of the power and the allies."

"What is the third position?"

"This is the way of the traditional Indian medicine men. Rather than just witnessing the nagual, they use it for healing, they get information from it, they find healing herbs through their relationship to it. It is really incorrect, God is loving, to speak of the medicine man's relationship to "it". What don Juan calls power is seen by these Indians as a personality, the Great Spirit, the one who created all the world. The medicine men when they heal serve as a channel between the Great Spirit and the ailing members of their tribe. They mediate the interaction of the Healer and the patient."

"Ah! Now that's more like it," we say. "That speaks to our concerns more fully. If we could talk with them we could explore our scientific and religious questions and maybe even find a larger meaning for ourselves."

"This seems to be the way you should take. But your enthusiasm must be tempered by caution for this is a dangerous land. You must be careful. All three positions are viable choices. In particular, don't forget don Juan for he has brought many to the border where they may witness the nagual. If he has forgotten the Person at the center of it, he has still made his way, has found a path with heart. You too must seek a path with heart, constantly asking if your particular way has a heart for you.

"We will walk with you a little way showing you where to go to find the medicine men. Then you will go on on your own. Your canteen is full and here is some fruit. If you are careful you will easily make it to the Indians with these supplies. Always remember to offer a drop of water and a bit of fruit to the desert. In this way, it will become your friend. Come, Ruth, it is time to leave."

The three of us set out together. Ruth walks ahead, leading the way. Moses is on my left. For a long time, no one speaks. Ruth stops and turns to us and we catch up with her. She points into the distance where we see puffs of smoke rising in several places.

Moses speaks. "This is where we leave you. Go and with God's grace you will arrive. Continue in line with the sun and you will make it in one day. Perhaps some time we will meet again."

Ruth looks at us knowingly and her eyes seem to smile. Then the two of them turn and walk back the way we had come. As they grow smaller, we are again alone but more hopeful now and we start our walk to the Indians.

Though our feet continue their straight journey, our mind heads in many directions at once. Moses and Ruth have disappeared as quickly as the mirages, though the fruit in our pouch assures us of the reality of that meeting. And we didn't even thank them! Such is our gratitude at being found when we were lost. Ruth remains an enigma. Had it been solely up to us we might rather have gone with her than to the unknown Indians. Medicine men! Of all people to meet on our journey to the Word. Our initial question, however, did suggest that an answer might be found in the interconnection between

Chapter 2

The Indian Medicine Men—A Possibility

science and religion and these healers, if Moses is right, do just that, for their religious healing is a science itself. Connect the patient with the Great Healer by channeling the healing forces into the sick one. And yet, our scientific side is skeptical. How can healing come from a place which isn't, from something we usually deny? Don Juan would probably remind us that our perception of the world is just a construction, that there is another world. In many ways, it is surprising that we have chosen the medicine men rather than don Juan for his approach to the nagual better fits our skepticism. We might

translate his witnessing into these terms: "There is much about reality which we do not yet understand, which is thus wonderful and terrifying. We can expect nothing magical from this world but it is all right to be amazed by it." Still there is a suspicion that don Juan would laugh at our translation.

Our choice suggests that there is something beyond our skepticism operating at a deeper level within us. It is this which searches for meaning, having left our comfortable city and then our mountain chalet. Beyond the skepticism is the hope that there is a central meaning in life, the Word perhaps, which weaves it all together.

At the same time, the skepticism will not be denied. What, it asks, do you know now that you didn't know before you left the mountains? Do you really expect to find meaning with some superstitious Indians who work magic tricks on their tribe members? Don Juan admitted that he tricked Castaneda but Castaneda considered the trickery valuable.

We have chosen to visit the medicine men and our thoughts now fall into step with our feet. The medicine men know a person, the Great Spirit, who brings healing and meaning. If we are to take this journey at all we may just as well remain open to what they will show us. Certainly we can count on our skepticism to flare and ask all the "appropriate" questions. Really, we may find out something. For the first time in a long while we notice a bounce in our step and an eagerness in our heart.

Finally, we come to an Indian village. This last has not been a hard journey at all. There is water still in our canteen and fruit in our pouch. A young Indian greets us and we tell him what has happened and what we seek. He runs into the center of the village and when he returns he says that a powwow will be held for us and that we are fortunate that the Great Spirit has brought many great medicine men to the village to join us.

Soon several of us sit in a circle, the sacred hoop, around a blazing fire and pass the sacred pipe among ourselves. Two of

16

our old Indian companions chant quietly, then we are still for some moments. Each of the medicine men then acknowledges the importance of the pipe. Black Elk relates the myth of the giving of the pipe to the Indians (Neihardt, pp. 3ff.). All nod in agreement with Lame Deer who says that, "power flows down through that smoke, through the stem. The pipe is not a thing, it is alive for us" (Lame Deer, p. 12).

We interrupt. "Don Juan also speaks of power. What is this power?"

"No good thing can be done by any man alone," says Black Elk. "I first make an offering and send a voice to the Spirit of the World, that it may help me be true" (Neihardt, p. 2). "The spirits told me that I should do my duty among the Oglalas [his people] with the power they had brought me in visions" (Neihardt, p. 182).

Lame Deer then speaks of his desire when he was young to be a medicine man, emphasizing that becoming a medicine man is no rational decision. "But you cannot learn to be a medicine man by going to school. An old holy man can teach you about herbs and ceremonies . . . These things you can learn. But by themselves these things mean nothing. Without the vision and the power this learning will do no good. It would not make me a medicine man" (Lame Deer, p. 13).

"It seems that you're saying that power comes from the Great Spirit to you through your pipe and your visions, that the Great Spirit sends power to bring healing."

Rolling Thunder answers, "This spiritual power is supposed to be used in a good way and to help people, and I don't mean just sick people either. You can use it to help keep people from getting sick; you can use it for friendship and for good feeling among your family and among people wherever you go" (Boyd, p. 11).

"Then there are both teachings and power which help you to relate and to heal. But how are these two connected?" we ask.

"First of all," Rolling Thunder begins, "the teachings don't

17

come like some people think. You can't just sit down and talk about the truth. It doesn't work that way. You have to live it . . . and it don't come easy. . . . People are anxious to learn but not to do the discipline or purification. . . . These days people want everything in a hurry and then want it without much effort. That's why they miss out on a lot of things" (Boyd, p. 39, 214, 59).

Lame Deer talks now of the peyote religion, saying that it is something new, not one of the ancient, native beliefs. "I was once part of the peyote cult, but I stopped a long time ago. A man cannot be forever two things at one and the same time. So I cannot be a yuwipi, a true Lakota medicine man, and take peyote at the same time. It is also that my ideas about drugs have changed. Not that peyote is a drug—it is a natural plant. But as I see it now, as I feel it, I want my visions to come out of my own juices, by my own effort—the hard, ancient way. I mistrust visions come by in the easy way—by swallowing something. The real insight, the great ecstasy does not come from this" (Lame Deer, p. 216-217).

"Then taking peyote is bad?" we ask.

"Peyote is for poor people. . . . Once you have experienced the real thing you will never be satisfied with anything else" (Lame Deer, p. 65).

Rolling Thunder agrees that peyote is not a drug but a sacred agent. The taking of peyote is "a purification ceremony like most of our ceremonies. It's not used to get high or for foolishness. It's used in a way that we want to cleanse our systems and our minds, so we can put ourselves on a higher plane of life" (Boyd, p. 247). There is a pause. "Some of these people interested in ecology want to protect the earth, and yet they will cram anything into their mouths just for tripping or for freaking out—even using some of our sacred agents. Some of these things I call helpers; and they are taken very, very seriously, but they have to be used in the right way" (Boyd, p. 51).

"How does one learn to use these agents or the sacred herbs

or the power in the right way? Isn't the power always good?"

"No!" Rolling Thunder answers emphatically. "The same principles are always at work—the same techniques—and they can be used for good purposes or for bad. So there's good medicine and bad medicine. This idea that I've found in some modern people that there's no good or bad, that it's all the same, is pure nonsense. There's good and there's bad and they'd better know it" (Boyd, p. 198-199). He then tells us that only through the Great Spirit is the power good.

Black Elk adds, "Visions and ceremonies only make me like a hole, through which the power can come. If I thought I was doing it myself, the hole would close up and no power could come through" (Neihardt, p. 208-209).

"But not everyone has these powers. How does one come to get them? We know that you say by experience. How does one get to that experience?"

"I am made for it," Lame Deer says. "I am a medicine man because a dream told me to be one" (Lame Deer, p. 137, 158).

"I had a Great Vision," Black Elk says. (Neihardt, p. 20ff.)

"I was born to be a medicine man," Rolling Thunder adds. (Boyd, p. 6)

"Could you be more specific?" we ask.

Another silence follows but with a strange effect on us. It is as though the medicine men are communicating on a level which needs no words. Finally, as though an agreement has been made, Lame Deer speaks.

"I was alone on the hilltop. I sat there in the vision pit . . . left there for four days and nights without food or water until old man Chest, the medicine man came back for me . . . I was sixteen then, still had my boy's name and let me tell you, I was scared. When it was all over I would no longer be a boy, but a man. I would have had my vision. . . . Old man Chest had wrapped the star blanket around me to cover my nakedness. . . . If Wakan Tanka, the Great Spirit, would give me the vision and the power, I would become a medicine man. . . . The old medicine man had also left a peace pipe with me, together with a bag of tobacco. This pipe was even more of a friend to me than my star blanket. To us the pipe is like an open Bible. . . . There is just the pipe, the earth we sit on and the open sky. The spirit is everywhere . . . As I ran my fingers along the pipe's bowl, I no longer felt scared . . . I sensed that my forefathers who had once smoked this pipe were with me on the hill. . . . I was no longer alone. . . . I wanted to become a medicine man, a yuwipi, a healer. But you cannot learn to be a medicine man like a white man going to medical school. An old holy man can teach you about herbs and ceremonies . . . But by themselves these things mean nothing. Without the vision and the power this learning will do no good. . . . Night was coming on. I was still lightheaded and dizzy from my first sweat bath. . . . The sweat bath seemed to have made my brains empty. . . . Suddenly I felt an overwhelming presence. Down there with me in my cramped hole was a big bird. I could hear his cries and feel his feathers. This feeling was so overwhelming that it was just too much for me. . . . I took the sacred pipe and began to sing and pray: 'Tunkashila, grandfather spirit, help me.' But this did not help. . . . I was no longer myself. I started to cry. . . . I used long ago words in my prayer. . . . Slowly I perceived that a voice, a bird's cry, was trying to tell me something. . . . I heard a human voice too, a voice which could not come from an ordinary, living being. All at once I was way up there with the birds. . . . The earth and the stars were moving below me. A voice said, 'You are sacrificing yourself here to be a medicine man. In time you will be one. We are the fowl people . . . You are going to understand us whenever you come to seek a vision here on this hill.' . . . I felt that these voices were good, and slowly my fear left me. I had lost all sense of time. . . . I felt the power surge through me like a flood. . . . I didn't know how long I had been up on that hill, one minute or a lifetime. . . . Chest came for me and told me that the vision pit had changed me in a way that I would not be able to understand for awhile. He told me also that I was no longer a boy, that I was a man now. I was Lame Deer" (Lame Deer, p. 11-16).

Lame Deer sits directly across from us. As he finishes he stares into the fire. Whether by the magic of the fire, the desert eeriness, or the spirit within the sacred hoop, all is silence. And not the empty silence but the world which exists behind the sound of the ear crickets. What he says seems possible, believable. In fact, this world of Lame Deer's surrounds us, as though ready to pounce on us, to burst into our reality. Slowly, the fear of the pit creeps over us. We feel our neck stiffening, freezing. Perhaps this is so the big bird can get us from behind. We too slip into a timelessness. Our thoughts overlap and weave in with each other suggesting different possibilities. A voice is speaking to us, pulling us forward. As in a dream, we notice that Black Elk is speaking as he stares at us. We don't know how long he has been talking or what important things we have missed. Torn, we want to go back and yet we are grateful to Black Elk for calling to us, perhaps saving us from the fowl people.

". . . Now and then the voices would come back when I was out alone, like someone calling me. . . . It was the summer when I was nine years old. . . . While I was eating one day with Man Hip, a voice came and said: "It is time; now they are calling you." The voice was so loud and clear that I believed it . . . The next morning I was very sick. . . . I was lying in our tepee and my mother and father were sitting beside me. I could see out through the opening, and there two men were coming from the clouds. . . . Each carried a long spear and from the points of these a jagged lightning flashed. They came clear down to the ground and stood a little way off and said: 'Hurry! Come! Your Grandfathers are calling you!' . . . They left the ground like arrows . . . a little cloud was coming. It stooped and took me to where it came from, fast. . . . Then there was nothing but the air and the little cloud. . . . The three of us were there alone in the middle of a great white plain . . . it was very still. . . . I saw a bay horse and he spoke:

21

'Behold me!' . . . Then there were twelve black horses of the west. . . . Their manes were lightning and there was thunder in their nostrils . . . there were twelve white horses of the north all abreast . . . and twelve sorrel of the east . . . and twelve buckskins of the south. . . . And when I had seen all these, the bay horse said: 'Your Grandfathers are having a council. These shall take you; so have courage.' . . . There was a heaped up cloud ahead that changed into a tepee and a rainbow was the open door of it. . . . I saw six old men sitting in a row. . . . The oldest of the Grandfathers spoke with a kind voice: 'Come right in and do not fear. . . . Your Grandfathers have called you here to teach you.' . . . I shook all over with fear now, for I knew that these were not old men, but the Powers of the World, the powers of the West, East, North, South, Sky and Earth. . . . The first Grandfather showed me the thunder beings and he spoke of understanding. I saw the rainbow leap with flames of many colors over me. He gave me a wooden cup filled with water and said: 'It is the power to make live and it is yours.' Now he had a bow. 'Take this. It is the power to destroy and it is yours.' And each of the Grandfathers gave to me and told me to take courage. With the sacred pipe, the third Grandfather said 'With this you shall walk upon the earth, and whatever sickens there you will make well.' . . . I was given visions about the future of my people. . . . I did battle and saw many places . . . with the horses and with my people. . . . After many visions, the two men were coming from the east. . . . They came and gave an herb to me and said: 'With this on earth you shall undertake anything and do it.' It was the day-break-star herb, the herb of understanding and they told me to drop it on the earth . . . it grew and flowered, four blossoms on one stem, a blue, a white, a scarlet, and a yellow and the rays from these streamed upward to the heavens so that all creatures saw it and in no place was there darkness. . . . And I saw the six Grandfathers and they cried 'He has triumphed!' . . . Each gave the gift he had given before—the cup of water and the bow and arrows;

the power to make live and to destroy; the white wing of cleansing and the healing herb; the sacred pipe; the flowering stick. . . . Then the oldest of them said: 'Grandson, all over the universe you have seen. Now you shall go back with power to the place from whence you came. . . . The tepee began to sway back and forth and the flaming rainbow door was growing dimmer. . . . I went through the door . . . and I walked alone amidst the singing of all kinds of voices. . . . When the singing stopped, I was feeling lost and very lonely. . . . I walked very fast, for I was homesick now. Then I saw my own tepee, and inside I saw my mother and my father bending over a sick boy that was myself. And as I entered the tepee, some one was saying: 'The boy is coming to! . . . Then I was sitting up; and I was sad because my mother and my father didn't seem to know I had been so far away."

Black Elk has finished speaking. It is suddenly cold and we are covered with gooseflesh. We move closer to the fire, as did Icarus, but we are warmed, not burned. We gather together our courage and proceed.

"Once you have received your call and become a medicine man, how does the actual healing take place?"

Black Elk and Hosteen Klah (Newcomb, 1964) both remind us that becoming a medicine man takes years of training, that one isn't ready to cure merely because of his vision. Black Elk (Neihardt, p. 208) tells us that the medicine man needs to perform his vision before his people to get its power.

"Then the people are important factors in their own healing?" we ask.

"It is up to the person," Lame Deer says (p. 211). "If he wants to be cured, he will be cured."

Rolling Thunder agrees (Boyd, p. 58) that there is a law of invocation and response. "One cannot be helped until he seeks help."

"Then the person's attitude is more important than the herbs?"

"You can take a glass of water and pray over it and make

23

medicine out of it," Rolling Thunder answers (Boyd, p. 9).

"Incredible! Has this been subjected to experimental testing?" asks that scientific part of our nature.

Rolling Thunder looks sternly at us. "The healing ritual is not a test but a helping of someone who is ill or injured." (Boyd, p. 205)

"What are some of the specific functions of the Indian medicine man among his people?"

Lame Deer answers: "I wish there were better words to make clear what 'medicine man' stands for but I can't find any. We have different names for different men doing different things for which you have only that one puny name. First we distinguish the healer—pejuta wicasa—the man of herbs. He does not cure with the herbs alone; he must also have the wakan power to heal. Then we have the yuwipi, the tied-one, the man who uses the power of the rawhide and the stones to find and to cure. We also speak of the waayatan—the man of vision who can foretell events which will happen in the future. Then there is the wapiya—the conjurer, the witch doctor. If he is good, he shoots at the disease, drawing up and sucking out of your body evil things. If he is bad he can cause sickness himself which only he can cure, for a price. . . . Another kind of medicine man is the heyoka—the sacred clown—who uses his thunder power to cure people. But the more I think about it, the more I believe that the only real medicine man is the wicasa wakan—the holy man. Such a one can cure, prophesy, talk to the herbs . . . but all of this is of no great importance to him. These are merely stages he has passed through. He has the wakanya wowanyanke—the great vision. . . . This kind of medicine man is neither good nor bad—he lives. . . . All medicine men have their own personal ways of acting according to their visions. The Great Spirit wants people to be different" (Lame Deer, pp. 154-156).

"Then being a medicine man implies more than healing?"

"I believe," Lame Deer answers (p. 153) "that being a medicine man, more than anything else, is a state of mind, a way of looking at and understanding this earth, a sense of what it is all about."

"It is understanding then which is most crucial?"

"It is from understanding that power comes," Black Elk says (Neihardt, p. 212).

"There is a contradiction. Earlier Lame Deer said that the power was the important thing not the studying and the knowledge."

Rolling Thunder smiles. "Not all knowledge can be put in books" (Boyd, p. 259). After a pause, "Understanding begins with love and respect. It begins with respect for the Great Spirit" (p. 52).

"In a vision I heard a voice," Lame Deer adds (p. 137). "It said 'You have love for all that has been placed on this earth, not like the love of a mother for her son, or of a son for his mother, but a bigger love which encompasses the whole earth. You are just a human being, afraid, weeping under that blanket, but there is a great space within you to be filled with that love. All of nature can fit in there.' "

"You are speaking of something which you know in your world, Lame Deer, that we do not know in ours."

"We Indians live in a world of symbols and images where the spiritual and the commonplace are one. . . . From birth to death, we Indians are enfolded in symbols" (Lame Deer, p. 109-113)

"What symbols?"

"The Indian symbol is the hoop, for nature wants all things to be round" (Lame Deer, p. 112).

"All life is a circle, the Great Spirit's emblem;" Rolling Thunder says (Boyd, p. 266).

A tear rolls down Black Elk's cheek, "And I, to whom so great a vision was given in my youth—you see now a pitiful old man who has done nothing, for the nation's hoop is broken and scattered. There is no center any longer, and the sacred hoop is dead" (Neihardt, p. 276).

A tear of our own answers his. A deep longing for an unknown long ago wells up within us. That all-saying wail of the desert, of us, mingles with the chant that has begun again. The sacred pipe is again passed among us and we smoke. Black Elk rises, then Lame Deer and Rolling Thunder, Hosteen Klah who has said little and another Indian that we don't know. The other white people who are with us then stand, an old, old man, a middle aged woman and two younger men. The fire has burned out and the Indians slip into the darkness. The hoop is broken.

Walking away, the woman and one of the young men join us. After the silence which happens so naturally in the desert, we speak with each other. It soon is obvious that these two have much to tell. The woman shares with us her long relationship with Hosteen Klah, the healings that she witnessed, his chants and the Navaho sand painting. She then relates an incredible story of his power.

"The next day being Saturday" she begins "a day off for the girls, we could accompany Arthur [her husband] and Klah back to the Reservation. . . . The morning was cloudy with blustery fall winds, so we started early. . . . We had gone about forty miles when heavy, wind-blown clouds darkened the sky and hard gusts made driving difficult. Suddenly I looked across the mesa to my right and exclaimed, 'What's that?' Everyone looked that way and Arthur said 'It's a cyclone!' He stopped the car and we watched the black hourglass column as it spun and swayed on a path that would take it across the road about a half-mile in front of us. We were already beginning to feel the sidewinds sucking in toward the center, when, to our horror, it turned directly toward us. We had all been standing in front of the car watching the progress of the funnel; now I told the girls to hurry and rushed to climb into the car. But not Klah. He started walking slowly toward the whirling mass, which was approaching with the sound of a thousand swarming bees. Stooping now and then to pick up a pinch of earth or part of a desert plant, he put the accumulation into his mouth while he was chanting. We could not very

26

well turn around and go away, leaving him to face the tornado alone, and anyway, it was now much too late to make our escape, so we simply sat there—four of the most frightened humans anybody ever knew. Klah continued to walk slowly into the eddying wind, then suddenly held up both hands and spewed the mixture in his mouth directly at the approaching column and raised his voice to a loud chant. The column stood still for a moment and then divided in the center of the hourglass, the upper part rising to be obscured by the low hanging clouds and the lower half spinning away at right angles to its former course like a great upside down top.

"Klah turned around and came back to the car. Had we witnessed a miracle of faith? To this day, I believe we did. Later I asked Klah about the plants and the soil he had picked up, and he said, 'The Spirit of the Earth is more powerful than the Wind Spirit.' " (Newcomb, p. 198-199).

"Impossible!", we say after she finishes but we laugh, more open than ever to the impossibilities being told.

Then the young man speaks. "I'll now tell you a story about Rolling Thunder. We were leaving for the last interview before a conference we were attending in San Francisco . . . Rolling Thunder had gotten up at the last minute. We wanted to give him breakfast. It was all too fast for him, and he left the house without his tobacco. He realized this as we drove through Berkeley. I saw him reach into a pocket of his sports coat, take out his pipe, and reach into the pocket again. He picked up the coat, put his hand into another pocket and then another. He stretched his legs and checked his pants pockets. Suddenly he waved his arm through the air and snapped his fingers loudly.

" 'What's the matter?', asked Buffalo Horse, his son.

" 'I've forgotten my pipe tobacco!' He began to go through the pockets again. 'It can't be in here,' said Rolling Thunder. 'We just came out and got in the car a few minutes ago.'

"After Buffalo Horse checked the coat pockets again, Rolling Thunder said, 'Look, the tobacco's not here. It's in the bedroom in the house. I know exactly where the tobacco is; it's on that little table with the bumpy stone top.'

" 'Do you want to go back?'

" 'We can't. We'd never make it to the interview.'

"I knew the tobacco was important. Rolling Thunder had always used his pipe for rituals and ceremonies or whenever he was in deep thought or was planning. . . . He said nothing on the way to San Francisco. He just stared out the window. . . . We arrived in the parking lot, and looked for a parking place. Rolling Thunder still did not speak. I could not believe he was nervous about the program; he had never been nervous before. I knew he was not a habitual tobacco user, but his pipe may have been really necessary now. I wondered if he was upset about having rushed off without his tobacco. Perhaps he was just enjoying the morning? I could not see his face from the back seat, and I hoped he was all right.

"As I began to speak he snapped, 'I've got it! All right! I've got it right here!' The tobacco pouch was in his hand! 'I knew right where it was. It's not hard when you know where it is. These things can be done. When there's a need for it, it can be done.'

"It was difficult for my mind to accept that Rolling Thunder had just 'brought' his pouch of tobacco into the moving car from the little bedside table across the bay. Still I did believe it. My knowledge that the tobacco had not been in the car and my knowledge of Rolling Thunder were much more certain than my knowledge that such things are impossible" (Boyd, p. 255-257).

At this point, we go our separate ways, saying nothing more. A mind can handle only so much bending at once. Soon we are totally alone, the black desert having completely surrounded us. In this personal silence, our mind tries in vain to regroup, to find the weaving thread of this star blanket fantasy. Don Juan comes to our aid. A trick. Of course, it's all a sorcerer's trick. But why did these several Indians and their white friends join forces to bring this trick off? And the healings. A good trick indeed which could cause them. Trick the different body systems into repairing the unrepairable. Or the seemingly unrepairable. Ah, there's a mechanism which we only don't understand as yet. This thought reassures us. But only for a moment, for a residue remains from our discussions. Maybe we don't have a corner on the understanding market after all. Maybe the Great Spirit does empower these healers. Maybe we've been avoiding that part of ourselves which we fear. A little voice whispers just below a sensibly audible level, our own meager vision. "One day you may be spiritually ill and need someone like Black Elk or Rolling Thunder to put you in touch with the Great Spirit. It's then that you will need to believe." And somehow, it is this voice, this un-vision, which pushes us onward, which involves us in our own questions more seriously, which makes us want to know.

Chapter 3 *Shamans — Everyone but Us*

Thankfully, we have escaped the desert. As it had done before, our mind readjusts itself to our experience. Questions occur to us which had not when we were with the Indians. Simply put, we have been much too polite, not pursuing the truth in a scientific manner. Some of the questions, however, were not intended for them anyway, needing instead to be subjected to a new exploration. Why, for instance, is such truth isolated in one locale? After all, weren't the Indians really a group of superstitious savages who were civilized by white colonizers? This assumption works for a moment until

we are again swamped by a rush of memories. . . . Hosteen
Klah taming the tornado (witnessed after all by four civilized
folks) . . . the appearance of Rolling Thunder's tobacco in the
car (a charming impossibility at the least) . . . the great visions
and the healings . . . the openness to Wakan Tanka, the Great
Spirit . . . the end of the power and Black Elk's tears of
despair, for the hoop is broken. . . . Not only does our col-
onizing assumption seem heartless; it also is less than scientific, at least for its automatic exclusion of such facts. There's
something to this, the medicine and the Great Spirit and the

power but . . .

The question remains. Why the isolation in the American desert of these truths? A simple answer, something along the line of a chosen people would satisfy but such is not our fate. Less than surprised by now, we find as we search that the isolation exists only in our minds for everywhere we look there are similar stories being told. For a moment, we feel totally uprooted, separated from our initial question which had something to do with science and religion. Replacing the question is a feeling of embarrassment at our obvious hubris. How have we gotten ourselves so far afield? But the two sides of our nature come to our aid. Science says, "Now that we're here, shouldn't we explore the territory?" And religion, "Something powerful is about. We have no choice, having begun, but to pursue it." With this, our footing is somewhat reestablished and we go on.

One man in particular helps us at this point in our investigation. He has known many shamans and friends of shamans and he provides us with our information about them. As we recall our journey so far, he smiles and tells us, "All the world over, magico-religious powers are held to be obtainable spontaneously . . . or deliberately" (Eliade, p. 22).

The Indian medicine men told us of their special selection by the Great Spirit to be healers. How is it with these others, the shamans?"

Shamans are of the 'elect' and as such they have access to a region of the sacred inaccessible to the other members of the community. . . . The shaman begins his new, his true life by a 'separation' . . . by a spiritual crisis that is not lacking in tragic greatness and in beauty" (p. 7, 13).

"Then, as with the Indians, the shaman is chosen by the Spirit?"

"A shaman is not recognized as such until after he has received two kinds of teaching, (1) ecstatic (dreams, trances, etc.); and (2) traditional (shamanic techniques, the names and functions of the spirits, etc)" (p. 13).

"What are these ecstatic experiences like?"

"The content of the first ecstatic experiences . . . almost always includes one or more of the following themes: dismemberment of the body, followed by renewal of the internal organs and viscera; ascent to the sky and dialogue with the gods or spirits; descent to the underworld and conversation with the spirits of dead shamans; various revelations, both religious and shamanic (secrets of the profession)" (p. 34).

"Can you give examples of specific ecstatic visions of these shamans? Are they like those of the Indian medicine men?"

"Among the Yakut, the future shaman 'dies' and lies in the yurt for three days without eating or drinking. . . . The candidate's limbs are removed and disjointed with an iron hook; the bones are cleaned, the flesh scraped, the body fluids thrown away, and the eyes torn from their sockets . . . the bones are gathered together and fastened with iron . . . each [Yakut] shaman has a Bird-of-Prey-Mother, which is like a great bird with an iron beak, hooked claws and a long tail. This mythical bird shows itself only twice: at the shaman's spiritual birth and at his death. [It] takes his soul, carries it to the underworld, leaves it to ripen on a branch of a pitch pine. When the soul has reached maturity the bird carries it back to earth, cuts the candidate's body to bits, and distributes them among the evil spirits of disease and death. Each spirit devours the part of the body that is his share; this gives the future shaman power to cure the corresponding diseases. The Bird-Mother restores the bones to their places and the candidate wakes as from a deep sleep" (p. 35-36).

"Among the Ammasalik Eskimo, the shaman himself chooses the candidate in his early childhood. The old angakok [shaman] finds a pupil and the teaching is conducted in the deepest secrecy, far from the hut, in the mountains. The angakok teaches him to isolate himself in a lonely place—beside an old grave, by a lake—and there rub two stones together while waiting for a significant event. 'Then, the bear of the lake or inland glacier will come out, he will devour all your flesh . . .

33

you will awaken and your clothes will come rushing to you' . . . the Eskimo neophyte must undergo an initiatory ordeal. Success in obtaining this experience requires his making a long effort of physical privation and mental contemplation directed to gaining *the ability to see himself as a skeleton.* 'Though no shaman can explain to himself how and why, he can, by the power his brain derives from the supernatural . . . divest his body of its flesh and blood, so that nothing remains but his bones. And he must then name all parts of his body, mentioning every single bone by name . . . By thus seeing himself naked, altogether freed from the perishable and transient flesh and blood, he consecrates himslf, in the sacred tongue of the shamans . . .' To reduce oneself to this skeleton condition is equivalent to re-entering the womb of this primordial life, that is, to a complete renewal, to a mystical rebirth" (pp. 58-63).

"Having heard of several of these kinds of experiences, it's hard not to notice their similarity to severe psychological disturbances."

Eliade agrees: "That such maladies [as hysteria, anxiety, epileptoid seizures] nearly always appear in relation to the vocation of medicine men is not at all surprising. Like the sick man, the religious man is projected onto a vital plane that shows him the fundamental data of human existence. . . . But the primitive magician, the medicine man, or the shaman is not only a sick man; he is, above all, a sick man who has been cured" (p. 27).

"What is the cure which separates shamans from sick men?"

"[S]hamans . . . cannot be regarded as merely sick; their psychopathic experience has a theoretical content" (p. 31).

"And so?"

"It is only this twofold initiation—ecstatic and didactic—that transforms the candidate from a possible neurotic into a shaman recognized by his particular society" (p. 14).

"Then the shaman is special but not neurotic?"

"He is . . . a sick man who has been cured . . . what is

important to note is the singularization, by 'election,' by 'choice,' of those who experience the sacred with greater intensity than the rest of the community—those who, as it were, incarnate the sacred because they live it abundantly, or rather 'are lived' by the religious 'form' that has chosen them" (p. 27, 32).

"All these shamans claim to have experienced an inner or other world which is powerful, dangerous and potentially healing but their experiences often take relatively different forms."

"The process of sacralizing reality is the same; the forms taken by the process . . . differ . . . [Nothing] is final . . . the same individual can have an infinite variety of religious experiences . . . the dialectic of the sacred makes possible the spontaneous reversal of any religious position" (p. xvii, xviii).

"What about drugs? Some of the Indian medicine men speak of using them to bring about religious experience."

"Narcotics are only a vulgar substitute for 'pure' trance. . . . Narcotic intoxication is called on to provide an *imitation* of a state that the shaman is no longer capable of attaining otherwise" (p. 401).

"Then shamans should have access to this other inner world without using drugs?"

"[F]or certain religious consciousnesses in crisis, there is always the possibility of a historical leap that enables them to attain otherwise inaccessible spiritual positions" (p. xix).

Here conversation ends. His last statement, if true, is as applicable to us as to the medicine men and the shamans. That slipping we felt around the fire after Lame Deer's account . . . it could happen to us. . . .

But enough of this religious jabbering, says our empiric side. What is most noticeable is the utter difference between the point of view of these primitives and the generally accepted materialistic view of our own culture. Again, and in new form, the recurring question: if experiences such as these have been available and useful to practically every culture the world over, where have they gone within our culture? And why do they seem so foreign, so forbidden, so frightening, so impossible?

Chapter 4 *It's Lonely Here Now*

We're a bit surprised at this juncture for we've found out some things on our journey which would affirm our everyday attitude on one level and yet would profoundly alter it on another. Part of our accepted attitude has been that we moderns have taken an enormous step out of the cave of primitivism, that we have become enlightened, that we need no superstitious beliefs and finally, that we are alone and highest among cultures because of our enlightenment. The evidence of our journey so far would seem to agree and to disagree. Our experience (which is the measure used by both

our scientific and religious natures) suggests something more. Perhaps in our giant step we have left something behind, something very real, a reality which can be witnessed, used and even seen to have a purpose of its own which may run contrary to ours.

If only we search our mind we will recall why our attitude has won. For it has won; that much we know. But exploring the hidden regions of our mind we find only such words as "superstitious, impossible, failure to face reality, impossible." This leaves us more than a little ill at ease for, given our new experience, our new point of view if it may be called that, we see such words as non-scientific, non-empiric and worst of all, self-descriptive. For mustn't there be some superstitious failure to face reality which leads us to declare something impossible without even examining it?

There is again a sickening immediate lapse of reality, a dissolution of what we know. We swoon as we struggle to recreate, to recategorize our experience. An unforeseen terror invades us. It's only superstition, impossible, we think, trying to battle it. But we find ourselves empty handed, for how can we battle that which doesn't exist? Of course, of course, it doesn't exist, it's impossible, we say trying to collapse it but it breaks forth again, this impossible, this sickening floating dissociation. Ah, there! Crazy, that's it, this is crazy. The word surrounds it, crazy, crazy. Such terror is only crazy. But having experienced these crazy things we cannot forget them; what has happened is irreversible. Irreversible? Then what are we to do? We are orphaned, separated from our culture which has a word for it. Crazy. Oh not that! Not alone, not rejection by our lonely culture for it is all we have. Isn't it? Is it? There is the hint, the possibility, of something else. But how then have we gotten here? How gotten so separated from what these others, these shamans and medicine men claim as real? Is Black Elk right about being a hole for the spirit? Has our hole to the spirit closed in our attempt to be whole, to be contained? The painful contradiction of this strikes us. Our claim for wholeness has denied our wholeness by closing the hole to the holy. The Great Spirit, Wakan Tanka, Abba, has been excluded from our reality. No wonder we feel the angst, the dreadful loneliness. No wonder because we have no wonder.

A little voice, science, calls through to us: "But don't forget your experience. You still have your experience with which to view reality. Don't worry if the impossible occurs; we will just make room for it."

And another voice, religion, louder than science, for it now has the power: "It is impossible only because you deny it. If you open yourself to it, you will know its reality."

But what is *it*? Why are we so apart from *it*? How do we get to *it* and do we even want to, if *it* even is? It's superstition, yes, impossible, says our culture which has somehow gotten us where we are. If we can only find out how we have gotten here, it will all be explained, we will understand and we will arrive again, again enlightened to our old awareness. But a voice is speaking behind us.

"In most cultures from primitive ones to the developed cultures of China, India and Byzantine Christianity, non-physical realities have been seen as very important . . . the modern materialistic point of view sweeps away the highly developed attitudes of these peoples" (Kelsey, 1972, p. 42, 45).

Turning around we see him; a very strange coincidence, this, to meet him at this point on our journey.

"But how?" we ask in disbelief. "How did you know what we were thinking?"

"You were speaking out loud and I heard you as I was passing by," he answers.

"So what of this feeling of angst, of separateness?"

"You really didn't have much chance to feel any other way given the thinking of modern theologians. According to Macquarrie in his book *Twentieth Century Religious Thought*, only two men (Carl Jung and Baron von Hugel) of the more than 100 he analyzes clearly suggest that theological understanding requires a basis of some direct encounter with more than human reality and purpose. From the most liberal de-mythologizers to the most conservative fundamentalists the opinion is that God has no natural contact with individuals . . . the truth is that it is the great scientific minds of today who are far more open to a direct and natural experience of the divine than most of modern theology. Science's own discoveries, both within the atom and beyond our galaxy, have destroyed the mechanistic naturalism that had so little place for free men or their contact with more than human reality" (Kelsey, 1972, 27, 33, 36-37).

"But this science and theology seems backwards. How did things get in such a mess?"

"Not quite backwards perhaps. To understand we must take a look at how things got this way—which you were mentioning before I spoke to you. A way of doing this is to seek an answer to the question: How do we know the world? This is a question which has been asked again and again through the ages."

"Where does one begin?" we ask.

"As Heine said 'Plato and Aristotle. . . . Although under other names it is of Plato and Aristotle that we speak.' "

"What does this mean?"

"To understand how we know we need only go to these two men, for their different perceptions of ways of knowing have profoundly colored all Western thought after them. Plato, on the one hand, described three ways of knowing reality— through the senses, through the reason and through divine madness. Our senses tell us about sense reality, our reason interprets sense reality and gives us access to the intermediate mathematical reality, but only through the divine madness can men be in touch with the world of Ideas, the eternal" (1972, p. 52-53).

"Divine madness?"

"Plato understood that man could be in touch with the eternal in four ways: through prophesy, healing or catharsis, artistic inspiration and love" (1972, p. 53-55).

"He saw love as a way of knowing?"

"According to Plato, as a man's spirit is empowered by Love, as one is actually allowed to see and feel and love the beauty of another, one can be led on to the very idea of beauty and the good, to the mystical contemplation of God. This love, however, is not one in which the ego merges with the All as in Plotinus and Eastern mysticism but in which the ego remains distinct for Love implies an object" (1972, p. 55).

"How then did Aristotle see ways of knowing?"

"For him there were but two ways of knowing, through

sense experience and reason" (1972, p. 65).

"But what of divine madness?"

"There is no place for divine madness in Aristotle's system since then any simple person might have as direct access to truth as the most learned metaphysician . . . Aristotle realized that all information given by sense experience is subject to change, always uncertain and he was looking for some access to some certain knowledge. For this reason he favored the logical certainty of deductive reason over the tentative character of inductive thought. . . . One obtains knowledge not by divine inspiration but by human rationality" (1972, p. 65).

"Plato's approach seems more in line with the shamans and medicine men while Aristotle is closer to our modern way of thinking."

"But this wasn't always the accepted way. One could trace the changing of accepted attitudes about knowing from Plato right up to the present."

"Would you do that for us?" we ask.

"I'll give a sketch of the main thinkers in our tradition and their attitudes toward ways of knowing. First of all, it is important to know that Aristotle's approach to ways of knowing, to inner reality and to dreams had little popularity in the ancient world. For him, dreams were residual impressions of the day left on the soul and in his *Metaphysics* the dream was used as an example of the non-existent. Except for Cicero, most other ancient thinkers were in basic agreement with Plato about how we know reality" (1968, p. 67).

"What kind of implications did that have on the culture?"

"The attitude was reflected, for instance, in the medicine of the day. Hippocratic medicine used dreams for treatment of physical ailment. Dream interpretation lived side by side with the doctor's knowledge of his patient. Galen also treated patients successfully by remedies revealed in dreams. Incubation, or waiting for a dream to point the way to healing, was practiced in the temples of Asklepios. There was scarcely in ancient time any disagreement with the understanding that dreams were significant and related one to inner reality" (1968, p. 70-71).

"What of the other cultures?" we ask.

"Dreams play an important part in the Babylonian *Gilgamesh Epic*. Egyptians had a high regard for dreams and the inner world. Dreams and the inner world were also very important to the Hebrews" (1968, p. 45-46).

"What can you tell us of their attitude?"

"The Hebrews believed that Yahweh brought men special knowledge of the world, of divine reality through the dream. . . . The prophets were considered important religiously and politically because they had the power to see beyond the immediate world. . . . False prophets were to be put to death. The prophetic function of dreaming and interpreting was so important that to pervert it was a heinous offense and had to be punished by death" (1968, p. 18, 19, 31).

"Their relationship was so serious to a part of reality that we would deny."

"Yes. And the Book of Job, the Book of Daniel, the Talmud which devotes four chapters to dreams and the Kaballah point to their ongoing relationship to this reality and to the dream" (1968, p. 37, 42, 43).

"What about the Christian New Testament?"

"The people of the New Testament believed themselves to be in direct contact with the non-physical reality of the Spirit which saved them from other non-physical realities which were evil. One difference between the testaments is that the New Testament sees spiritual reality dualistically which is the Persian solution where the Old Testament for the most part sees all reality, good and evil, emanating from Yahweh" (1968, p. 97, 100).

"What kind of changes did this bring to men of the New Testament?"

"Perhaps the central feature was that the ordinary Christian in the classical Christian community could encounter divine reality, whereas in shamanistic religions and in the Old Testament this reality was open primarily to the shamans and the prophets" (1972, p. 48).

"The Christian attitude of those days would seem to have much in common with Plato's thinking."

"That's right. In fact, Christian theology in a modern sense began when Justin Martyr (c. 150 A.D.) realized that the philosophical ideas of Platonism gave an expression to what had been lived out and taught by Jesus of Nazareth. The other great Christian thinkers such as Tertullian, Origen, Ireneaus and Clement developed this line of thought (1972, p. 57; 1968, 107-111). Tertullian stated their attitude concisely: 'Now who is such a stranger to human experience as not sometimes to have perceived some truth in dreams?' (1968, p. 115). With Constantine, Christianity became acceptable and the state religion. Christians were freer and there were more heresies and more nominal Christians.

"The four great Doctors of the Eastern Church, Basil the Great, Gregory of Nazianzen, Gregory of Nyssa and Chrysostom, supported and further developed this platonic attitude. (1968, p. 133-142). The four great doctors of the West, Ambrose, Augustine, Jerome and Gregory the Great each taught in his own way that dreams and visions were one of God's methods of revelation to man. Ambrose stated his belief very clearly in his letter to the emperor Theodosius: 'I have been warned, not by man, nor through man but plainly by Himself that this (celebration of communion before the emperor) is forbidden me. For in the very night I was to set out you appeared to me in Church and I was not permitted to offer the sacrifice. . . .' God thus could affect the outer world through dreams according to Ambrose (1968, p. 144-147). Augustine's study of perception was as sophisticated as any in the ancient world. He saw reality as consisting of outer physical objects to which we react . . . and in addition to the realities that come from outer perception and from inner perception of memories, autonomous spiritual realities can present themselves directly to the inner eye (1968, p. 148-149).

According to Jerome, dreams were important but pagan practices such as incubation were out. Through the Latin Vulgate, however, Jerome listed dreams with soothsaying and the practice of listening to them was included with other superstitious ideas. Thus with him the changing attitude toward the inner world becomes obvious (1968, p. 153, 155). By the time of Gregory, Rome had fallen, the Western Empire no longer existed as such, Italy was overrun by the Goths and Lombards and partly conquered by the Emperor of Constantinople. Around Gregory were the growing ignorance and superstition of a dying culture. He admitted the validity of dreams on the one hand and warned in strong words of their danger on the other. Stating that dreams could arise from many sources he wrote that 'one ought to be very reluctant to put one's faith in the dream . . .' Gregory was torn between two attitudes and experiences, and as 'teacher of the Middle Ages' he passed on the same split. For six centuries the value of dreams was accepted with increasing credulity, and then with Aquinas, dreams were placed in an Aristotelian context and their value ignored and even forgotten by the Church" (1968, p. 158-161).

"All this history is a bit overwhelming," we say to him. "What you seem to be saying is that the Hebrews, Egyptians, Babylonians, Greeks and Romans except for Aristotle and Cicero, the Western Christians up to the Dark Ages and in some sense even up to Aquinas, and the Eastern Orthodox tradition all had known the importance of dreams and of the inner world. What happened with Aquinas that caused him to accept the Aristotelian framework?"

"Several things must be kept in mind if we are to understand Aquinas. Since about the fifth century few men in the Latin world read the basic Greek works of philosophy and science or the Greek fathers . . . It finally became almost a point of honor to be separated from things Greek and when the final break with Byzantium came in 1054, the Latin world went on its own way. Most understanding of former times that survived into the Middle Ages came through a few summaries. Boethius did translate Aristotle's logical works in the *Organon* but as for Plato practically nothing was known at first hand. Even Aquinas, superb scholar that he was, had never read the basic Platonic dialogues (1972, p. 63-64).

"The thinking of Aristotle was revived by the Arabs . . . This thought was undoubtedly one of the things that sparked the new Islamic civilization, and from there it swept into Europe soon after 1200. Aquinas saw some dangerous ideas being circulated, ideas that denied the value of the individual and so he began to study Aristotle himself. Aquinas became convinced of the truth of Aristotle's world view—particularly his view that man receives direct knowledge *only* through sense experience and reason. He set out to bring together the thought of Aristotle and the Church. Those parts which he couldn't resolve such as revelation he simply didn't discuss much (1972, p. 64-66).

"Neither Aquinas or Aristotle had any place for dreams in their philosophies for they both believed that this cast doubt on man's free will. Aquinas brought this thinking into the Church and it gradually became the acceptable thought of the Church. What is generally overlooked is the experience that Thomas had at the end of his life, a direct contact with the divine. When he was urged to go on he replied, 'I can do no more; such things have been revealed to me that all I have written seems as straw and I now await the end of my life.'" (1968, p. 173-177).

"So he had an experience of 'divine madness' himself?" we ask.

"It would certainly seem that he did. But the official doctrines of the church became shaped by his writings, rather than holding to his experience and so the ideal of certainty based on logic rather than experience became the chief cornerstone of theology and the church. The ideas of Aquinas did not win out immediately however. For years the Franciscans under the influence of Bonaventure—who were trying to integrate the thinking of Aristotle into the framework of Plato and Augustine—were forbidden to read Aquinas. Lesser scholastic thinkers took Aquinas' work and created a simplified dogmatic scheme. This systematic fusion of Aristotle and Biblical revelation was still regarded as unquestionable up to the Reformation. Luther broke away from it with his experience but didn't develop an integrative system of thought. Calvin's views were just as scholastic as those of Aquinas (1972, p. 67-68).

"It's also important to remember the basic world view or *Weltanschauung* of the time. The earth was seen as center of the universe. The heavenly bodies were understood to revolve in the epicycles of Ptolemaic astronomy. Space was seen as sensuous space extending outwardly indefinitely. And all this was known partly through sense experience, and more completely through man's supreme reason. Medieval man was at the center of things; he lived in a world which he understood" (1972, p. 68).

"Aquinas seems a remarkable thinker."

"His thinking *has* affected us radically . . . But let's continue. A lot of things began to happen. The revolution came. It began with Nicolaus Cusanus' questioning of the categories of Aristotle. It grew with the strange investigations of Paracelsus, the theorizing of Telesio and others. But the earthquake came with the findings of Nicholaus Copernicus who realized the radical nature of his work and refrained from publishing for fear of an accusation of heresy. But others brought out the discoveries which removed man from the center of the universe and called the entire Aristotelian world view into question. For the church such questioning was heretical since it cast doubts on the church's religious authority. The split between the questioning scientific spirit and the official church came to head with the burning of Giordano Bruno in 1600. Essentially, Bruno's sin was that he stood for the spirit of free inquiry over and against the authority of the establishment. The gulf widened as the church held on to its authority and the new science saw in religion nothing more than legal and intellectual restrictions" (1972, p. 70).

"Not unlike our present day," we add.

"Right. But there is a difference. A new one-sided world view was shaped by the science of the day, alienated from religion and tragically from the realities of inner experience. The scientists were left alone to expand their naturalistic and mechanical world. Only in modern times has a rapprochement begun but that comes later in our tale . . . Naturalistic science germinated and spawned. Kepler perfected Copernicus' theories showing that the heavenly bodies acted as any physical thing. Newton produced the brilliant mathematical and physical theories that showed the whole universe as one vast machine working according to precise mechanical laws. Finally, Darwin was convinced by his discoveries about evolution that man was a product of natural selection. Man rather than being the center of the universe was now one more outgrowth of a tiny and far from central bit of planetary matter" (1972, p. 70).

"Marx and Engels used Darwin's ideas for their materialism. For the church, the theory of evolution was another denial of the authority of the Bible. The idea of God working through the evolutionary process wasn't even considered and the battle continued and the church simply began to look foolish in the eyes of intelligent men. At the same time the mechanistic point of view had been popularized by Comte and Spenser and by the end of the nineteenth century was universally accepted. It was believed that man, by the exercise of his reason, had seized upon truth (1972, p. 71-72).

"But if one is to understand where modern theology and science are today, he must understand, at least in outline, the development of modern thought. Modern thinking takes off from the Aristotelian scholastic base in a quest for certainty. It was inaugurated by Descartes when he attempted to apply the model of analytical geometry to all experience in order to find solid ground for what we know. . . . His first premise was that of universal doubt. Anything unclear was eliminated. In

49

the famous *cogito ergo sum* (I think therefore I am), he demonstrated to *his* satisfaction the reality of his own subjective being, and he also derived the idea of viewing the reality of the subject as pure consciousness, or rational intellect. This was an entirely new idea which came to him along with his whole method in a triple dream experience on November 10, 1619. As L. L. Whyte has remarked, he made one of the great intellectual blunders of all time in so limiting the scope of human knowing that he excluded the source of his own inspiration" (1972, p. 73).

"Then unlike the Indians he closed the hole to the inner world and to divine madness."

"And others followed him down the path. In Thomas Hobbes' great deductive system most of the rationalistic conclusions of modern thinking were offered along with a disbelief in miracles since they did not fit in a rationalistic framework. After him, the empiricists stressed the place of empirical or sense experience. Locke held that the only sure knowledge was mathematical and all else must be derived empirically through sense experience. Berkeley proposed, contrary to the empiricists, that the material world was an idea in the mind of God but his thinking didn't carry the day. Hume carried the ideas of empiricism to their logical conclusion in ultimate skepticism by questioning the whole idea of efficient causality since man had no empirical evidence of cause and effect (1972, p. 73-74).

"Immanuel Kant came to believe not only that we have no certain knowledge of the external, physical world, but that we have no certain knowledge of the subjective mind either. He found man's reason to be the result and product of two unknown realities, a subjective thing-in-itself and an objective thing-in-itself. But he still followed Descartes' idea that thinking had to be clear and conscious. At the same time by denying the possibility that man's mind could come to any final knowledge, Kant also cast doubts on man's ability to know God through any logical process, showing where the deduct-

ive logical arguments of the scholastics broke down. The im-
pact of his thinking was and is tremendous. . . . The uncertainty of his thinking stimulated Hegel who believed by his
dialectic that he could obtain true and certain knowledge of
reality. For him, all reality was spiritual in content, everything was a manifestation of the absolute mind. But his system
left no place for the individual (1972, p. 74-75).

"Just preceding Kant and Hegel were two thinkers who
looked at the universe differently and who struggled to find
meaning in a mechanical universe. Spinoza concluded that the
universe was God or a force streaming from him. Leibniz, as
Einstein many many years later, saw force and substance as
identical. For him each individual is an idea of God, actualised
by means of a continual 'emanation' (1972, p. 75-76).

"There were also two violent reactions after Hegel to the
naturalism of the time. Kierkegaard demonstrated using
Hegel's method, that reason by itself could bring no religious
significance. He put the concrete individual experience above
Hegel's absolute mind. But his investigation was also rest-
ricted to immediate and physical reality. The individual was
thus again valued but never became aware of how much more
there was to personality than rationality and consciousness
(1972, p. 77-78). The opposite extreme is found in Nietzsche,
a prophet who didn't believe his prophecy" (p. 78).

"Would you say that his prophecy was a divine madness in a
Platonic sense?"

"Yes but Nietzsche could never reconcile himself to the
conflict between his naturalistic mind and his deeply religious
spirit. He saw the death of God presented by the naturalism
and the birth of the superman to fill the gap. He knew the
spiritual, inner world and having no place for it in his life, it
drove him mad (1972, p. 79).

"Entering our own century there was still a third reaction to
Hegel, found in the work of Husserl. He developed the
method of phenomenology and proposed to find absolute certainty and to make philosophy a science as solid as he thought

51

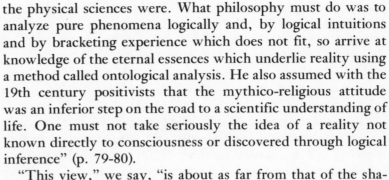

the physical sciences were. What philosophy must do was to analyze pure phenomena logically and, by logical intuitions and by bracketing experience which does not fit, so arrive at knowledge of the eternal essences which underlie reality using a method called ontological analysis. He also assumed with the 19th century positivists that the mythico-religious attitude was an inferior step on the road to a scientific understanding of life. One must not take seriously the idea of a reality not known directly to consciousness or discovered through logical inference" (p. 79-80).

"This view," we say, "is about as far from that of the shamans as one can get."

"And yet in various combinations, Kierkegaard, Nietzsche and Husserl are responsible for much European philosophical and theological thinking. Remember Macquarrie's finding that only Jung and von Hugel among more than 100 philosophers and theologians of the 20th century suggested the need for the direct encounter with more than human reality. The others had no place in their philosophy or theology for such an encounter. Heidigger, Marcel, Jaspers, Sartre, Merleau-Ponty, Bultmann, Bonhoffer, Tillich, Ritschl and Barth, none of them in their theology and philosophy saw the possibility of direct and consistent encounter with the inner spiritual world" (1972, p. 81-87, 27).

"Then as with Husserl, there was no possibility of direct contact with inner reality and meaning for any of them. It's an uncomfortable position to be in."

"Indeed. But the logical empiricists cast severe doubts upon the philosophizing of Husserl and his followers. The men of this school hold that the main task of philosophy is merely the analysis of language and experience and they maintain that nothing is meaningful which cannot be expressed in the language of physics. Language, as they see it, consists of words that refer to things and words which refer to relationships between things. All statements that are meaningful belong to natural science. All others are either tautological or meaningless. From this standpoint any statement about God or the Spirit which is not based on experience would be highly questionable" (1972, p. 90).

"Which allows experience a place again. But what of the scientists which you claim lead us out of the blind alley of modern theology?"

"That's another part of the story. Perhaps I might join you along part of the way and we may even meet some of these people who have again opened the door."

This prospect excites us and we agree. Before we go, we have some time alone and our mind explodes as it reviews the historical route we have taken. It refuses to order what it has heard in quite the way it was told. Rather it takes a different tack. What an incredible importance, it begins, is the culture and times of one's life. The first thousand years belong to Plato though it must be said that Aristotle's 'heresy' didn't get him burned. Rather it was Socrates who drank the hemlock. And in 1600, it looked like there might be a chance that science and religion could walk together (is that our question?) but the tension was better handled through a fire. Bruno's place seems strangely like that of the early Christians who met the lions, and the church the frightened Empire. Had Bruno lived in another time . . . but he didn't. The burning calls forth an inner fire. We suddenly no longer are the center of the universe and our solipsism is seen for what it is, a grand defense mechanism. The machine moves ever on. . . .

But where have we been? The shamans and medicine men, don Juan, Plato, the Hebrews, the Christian experience that everyone is a potential shaman, a hole, Plato and Christianity married, the Fathers, and darkness, the overrunning by the hordes, out of the darkness with Aristotle's Aquinas. What if instead of waiting for death, he had written some answer to himself? What if? Reformation, Luther's unsystematized experience and Calvin's unexperienced system, and the burning, and the split, a theology and philosophy grappling in the dark, split from science which proved the darkness, the bursting

53

minds which couldn't reassemble them. Perhaps it's better to run to one corner or the other for we're no longer the center anyway. Nietzsche, Friedrich. It won't come together. The scar tissue is too thick, the hole is healed, covered, though perhaps there's an infection. Do you see it? Friedrich, Crazy. Superman bursts into reality. Ego tries to be what Wakan Tanka is. Those Indians saying "If I thought it were me, the power wouldn't come through." Superman, Crazy. Friedrich can't bring it together for *it* doesn't fit with the naturalism of his day. Our being resonates with his, in horror. Is this the result of coming front and center, a crazy orphaned Superman? That's a more exact statement of our fear. So we deny it, philosophize, theologize it out of existence. It isn't acceptable culturally. But wait, that isn't the end of the story. The scientists are supposedly pointing to something else. It is time to move on, maybe in some impossible way to help Friedrich. It is time, though we are hardly going in the spirit of objective disinterest.

Chapter 5 The Scientists Construct a Bridge

We arrive at a large round building, a geodesic dome, and we are reminded of the sacred hoop although the dome sits at the edge of the ocean rather than in the desert. Several people are milling about while others move into the building. It seems to be a convention of some sort.

"Many people forget or don't acknowledge the things going on in this building," Kelsey says to us.

"Forget? What do you mean? We weren't even aware that this building existed."

"Which is what many would have you believe."

56

"But what has this to do with science or with the opening to the deeper world? What goes on here?"

"Since the first, almost simultaneous glimpses into the atom, into radiation, and into the psyche, in 1897, scientific thinkers here have shown the inadequacy of the 19th century world view in seven specific ways" (1972, p. 93).

"What ways?"

"The first three—the work that led to splitting the atom apart, the basic thinking of Einstein, and the development of quantum mechanics—changed man's whole view of time and

space and energy, and the implications have been thought through by the philosophy of science. Next, Godel challenged the very idea of mathematical certainty (which Locke said was the only certainty, we remember. Hume must be chuckling somewhere.) This was followed by new ideas about evolution and purpose. In medicine, men wrestling with some of man's most debilitating diseases found that man's body is deeply responsive to his emotions. Last, C. G. Jung gave evidence that man's most troublesome emotions could not be healed without a completely different view of the world, taking into consideration his contact with a creative center of meaning" (1972, p. 83).

"All that has gone on in there?" we ask pointing to the dome.

"Much of it has. Presently, a meeting is being held in which scientists and non-scientists are coming together to discuss these 20th century scientific ideas and their implications for individuals."

We walk in together and we're surprised for the building is impossibly large; it seems as though three times the space has been crammed into the building than the shell would suggest from outside. It is no orderly convention with a podium or area set aside for lectures. Rather, several little tables are set up throughout the room. At each table sit a few men and women talking while others rush between the tables. Many others are standing around in clusters. Some are gazing at the ceiling and we realize that we are in a large planetarium. Somehow, the lighting is such that though we stand in daylight below, we can clearly view the nightly heavens.

"Why not go join in one of the groups and get a feeling for what goes on here?" Kelsey suggests.

We move shyly into the group which is nearest to us. The men there smile a greeting which welcomes us. A discussion is in progress.

"Paradigms . . . are universally recognized scientific achievements that for a time provide model problems and so-

58

lutions to a community of practitioners. . . . Paradigms provide all phenomena except anomalies with a theory-determined place in the scientists' field of vision" (Kuhn, p. viii, 97).

"What are these anomalies you speak of?" one of the men on our side of the table asks.

"I'll give you an example," he answers. "Bruner and Postman did an experiment in which they inserted anomalous playing cards such as a red six of spades into a set of regular playing cards. These anomalous cards almost always were identified, without any hesitation or puzzlement, as normal. With a further increase of exposure to the anomalous cards, subjects did begin to hesitate and to display an awareness of anomaly. . . . Further increase of exposure to the anomalous cards resulted in still more hesitation and confusion until finally, and sometimes quite suddenly, most subjects would produce the correct identification without hesitation" (Kuhn, p. 63).

"But what can that have to do with science? Say, for instance with physics?" we ask, jumping in, eager to find out what scientists have to offer which will supposedly reconnect us with the inner world.

An old man, Heisenberg according to his name tag, responds: "It was in the theory of relativity that the necessity for a change in the fundamental principles, in the paradigm, of physics was recognized for the first time" (Heisenberg, p. 110).

"So that these new ideas or anomalies which the theory of relativity enabled scientists to discover entered into the scientific world?" We ask what seems obvious.

"Yes. But how difficult it is when we try to push new ideas into an old system of concepts belonging to an earlier philosophy—or to use an old metaphor, when we attempt to put new wine in old bottles" (Heisenberg, p. 139).

"Like the anomalous cards, Professor Kuhn?" the first man asks.

"Yes. And as Max Planck said 'A new scientific truth does not triumph by convincing its opponents and making them see the light, but rather because its opponents eventually die, and a new generation grows up that's familiar with it.' . . . In fact, the transfer of allegiance from paradigm to paradigm is a conversion experience that cannot be forced" (Kuhn, p. 151).

Conversion experience? By itself, that sounds much more like a religious notion than a scientific one. And new wine in old bottles, a direct quote from the New Testament. Perhaps our initial question *has* made some sense and religion and science may be closer together . . . but our mind is wandering. We return our attention to the conversation.

A man named Barnett is speaking: ". . . The human eye is sensitive to a very narrow range of the electromagnetic spectrum. . . . What man can perceive of the reality around him is distorted and enfeebled by the limitations of his organ of vision. . . . Realization that our whole knowledge of the universe is simply a residue of impressions clouded by our imperfect senses makes the quest for reality seem hopeless. . . . But a curious order runs through our perceptions, as if indeed there might be an underlayer of objective reality which our senses translate" (Barnett, p. 20-21).

"You're saying that what we are seeing is not reality but only a distortion?" asks the woman next to us.

Heisenberg answers, "We have to remember that what we observe is not nature itself but nature exposed to our method of questioning" (Heisenberg, p. 58).

"Wouldn't you rather say that we discover instruments which show us reality as it is?" we ask.

"Every tool carries with it the spirit by which it has been created. . . . The observation plays a decisive role in the event and the reality varies depending on whether we observe it or not" (Heisenberg, p. 27, 52).

"I don't understand," the first man says.

"Whenever one attempts to spy on the 'real' objective world, he changes and distorts its workings by the very process of his observation," Barnett answers. "According to Heisenberg's Principle of Uncertainty (he smiles at Heisenberg), a physicist can, for example, define electron behavior accurately as long as he is dealing with great numbers of them. When he tries to locate a particular electron the best he can say is that a certain point in the complex superimposed wave motions of the electron group represent the *probable* position of the electron in question. . . . Quantum physics thus shakes two pillars of old science, causality and determinism. . . . By dealing in terms of statistics and probabilities it abandons all idea that nature exhibits an inexorable sequence of cause and effect" (Barnett, p. 33-35).

Heisenberg adds, "The probability function combines objective and subjective elements. It contains statements about tendencies (potentia in Aristotelian philosophy) and these are completely objective; and it contains statements about our knowledge of this system which of course are subjective" (Heisenberg, p. 53).

"You talk as though the potentia are 'real' and what we know of them not real," a man who has just joined us says.

"I said objective and subjective, not real and unreal. . . . The transition from possible to actual takes place during the act of observation" (Heisenberg, p. 54).

"But the physicists don't know what they're actually seeing?" we ask.

"I believe that the language used by physicists when they speak about atomic events produces in their minds similar notions as the concept 'potentia'. So they have gradually become accustomed to considering the electromagnetic orbits, etc., not as reality but rather as a kind of 'potentia'. The language has already adjusted itself . . . but it is not a *precise language* in which one could use normal logical patterns; it is a language that produces pictures in our mind, but together with them the notion that the pictures have only a vague connection with reality, that they represent only a tendency toward reality" (Heisenberg, pp. 180-181).

"So that physicists communicate through a language which speaks in probabilities rather than in terms of the causality and determinism of earlier science?"

"One may say that atomic physics has turned science away from the materialistic trend of the 19th century. . . . It was in the theory of relativity that the necessity for a change was recognized for the first time as we said before. . . . The decisive change was in the structure of space and time which is very difficult to describe in the words of common language without the use of mathematics since the common words 'space' and 'time' refer to a structure of space and time that actually is an idealization and oversimplification of the real structure" (Heisenberg, p. 59, 110, 114).

"But didn't Godel show that even mathematics isn't certain?" we add.

"Right. During the whole period from the mathematicians of ancient Greece to the 19th century, Euclidean geometry had been considered as evident. . . . Then, the mathematicians Bolyai and Lobachevsky, Gauss and Riemann found that other geometrics could be invented which could be developed with the same mathematical precision as that of Euclid; therefore, the questions as to which geometry was correct turned out to be an empirical one. Einstein's work with space and time brought the problem into physics. . . . The theory of general relativity raised in an entirely new form the old questions of the behavior of space and time in the largest dimensions; it could suggest possible answers that could be checked by observations. . . . Consequently very old philosophic questions were raised about space and time" (Heisenberg, p. 123).

"This is baffling," we say to him.

"Only as you look at the world in terms of classical physics."

"But how then did classical physics get where it did?" someone asks from behind us.

"First, certain trends in Christian philosophy led to a very abstract concept of God. They put God so far above the world that one began to consider the world without at the same time seeing God in the world. . . . During the Renaissance, a new independent authority appeared—the authority of experience. . . . What we can see and touch became primarily real. . . . Matter was the primary reality. . . . This frame (besides being utilitarian) was so narrow and rigid that it was difficult to find a place in it for many concepts of our language that had always belonged to its very substance. . . . Mind was introduced only as a kind of mirror to the material world. . . . Even there one tried to apply the concepts of classical physics, primarily that of causality. . . . It was especially difficult to find in this framework room for those parts of reality that had been the object of traditional religion and seemed now more or less imaginary. . . . An open hostility of science toward religion developed. . . . Confidence in the scientific method and in rational thinking replaced all other safeguards of the human mind. . . . With modern physics we may say that the most important change brought about by its results consists in the dissolution of this rigid frame of concepts of the nineteenth century" (Heisenberg, p. 195-198).

"But what then is left?"

"One of the most important features of the development and analysis of modern physics is the experience that the concepts of natural language, vaguely defined as they are, seem to be more stable in the expansion of knowledge than the precise terms of scientific language. . . . This is in fact not surprising since these concepts are formed by the immediate connection with reality; they represent reality. . . . They never lose the immediate connection with reality. . . . Our attitude toward concepts like mind or the human soul or life or God will be different from those of the nineteenth century because these concepts belong to the natural language and have therefore immediate connection with reality. . . . We know that any understanding must be based finally upon the natural language because it is only there that one can be certain to touch reality, and hence we must be skeptical about any skepticism with regard to this natural language and its essential concepts. Therefore, we may use these concepts as they have been used at all times. In this way modern physics has perhaps opened the door to a wider outlook on the relation between the human mind and reality" (Heisenberg, p. 200-202).

"You mean that scientists now are open to the reality of God?" we ask incredulously.

Barnett and Heisenberg exchange a smile. We are reminded of Lame Deer and Rolling Thunder, the hoop.

Barnett speaks: "Einstein, one of the truly great modern scientists answered your question when he said 'The most beautiful and most profound emotion we can experience is the sensation of the mystical. It is the sower of all true science. He to whom this emotion is a stranger, who can no longer wonder and stand rapt in awe, is as good as dead. To know what is impenetrable to us really exists, manifesting itself as the highest wisdom and the most radiant beauty which our dull faculties can comprehend only in their most primitive forms—this knowledge, this feeling is at the center of religiousness' " (Barnett, p. 108).

"But we're speaking of science."

"On another occasion he declared: 'The cosmic religious experience is the strongest and noblest mainspring of scientific research' " (Barnett, p. 108).

Still another physicist, Dessauer, speaks: "Any scientist who has had the good fortune to be present at the birth of a great discovery or invention will never forget this experience. . . . Here it becomes perfectly plain that fulfillment can come to a man only after he has heeded certain requirements. Yet in many cases, and this is one of the profoundest of human experiences, it is the idea that takes hold of the man rather than the other way around. Man is overpowered by a relation, an insight. This, in a word, is revelation. . . . Man is a creature who depends entirely upon revelation. In all his intellectual endeavor, he should always listen, always be intent to hear and see. He should not strive to superimpose the structures of

64

his own mind, his systems of thought upon reality. . . . At the beginning of all spiritual endeavor stands humility, and he who loses it can achieve no other heights than the heights of disillusionment. . . . For man is in *statu viatoris*, in the condition of the wanderer. . . . Man is a wanderer and he has a compass if he hearkens to revelation. He senses the direction. But full arrival at the goal is denied to mortal life. . . . Each one of us, and each one of mankind, is a pilgrim to the absolute. And the Absolute is not an earthly possession but a mission. Man must not lose his orientation towards it; else he is confounded and falls into the abyss" (Dessauer, p. 319ff.).

Whoa! We leave the table feeling more than a bit overwhelmed. These scientists claim to have contact with an inner or spiritual reality which exists beyond the borders of our sensory and rational capabilities and yet the theologians seem to deny this reality. A strange state of affairs! It is as though the scientific-theological debate goes on but with the opponents in opposite corners than they were for several hundred years.

Dessauer describes our own position well, in *statu viatoris*, with humility, though the humility has been thrust upon us rather than being a completely free choice. But so it is. The scientists know the reality of which the Indians and shamans speak through revelation.

We see Kelsey standing at another table and we rush to tell him what we've heard. After we have done this, we ask him, "What is this revelation of which they speak?"

"The most dramatic suggestion," he answers, "has been made by the philosopher of science, Paul Feyerabend. He maintains that the crucial element in scientific discovery is not clear rational thought, but imagination. Without the capacity to imagine, to think in images, Feyerabend shows, the scientist has no way to perceive the structure of things as they are. Nor can he break out of his old conceptions, even when some new fact is staring him in the face. The way Albert Einstein arrived at his discoveries is certainly rather conclusive evi-

dence of this" (Kelsey, 1974, p. 104).

"How did he?"

"Einstein's reported remark to Jung is the classic description. Asked if he had to work very hard to produce his equations, Einstein smiled. 'Oh no,' he said. 'I meditate and the numbers dance before me.' " (1972, p. 131).

"The scientists seem to consider these images and ideas as real."

"They certainly do. For example, Godel sees mathematical concepts as realities of the same nature as Platonic ideas and says it this way 'Classes and concepts may . . . be conceived as real objects . . . existing independently of our definitions and constructions. It seems to me that the assumption of such objects is quite as legitimate as the assumption of physical bodies and there is quite as much reason to believe in their existence' " (Kelsey, 1972, p. 99).

"These are the first four. What of the other of the seven scientific breakthroughs you mentioned?"

"Another break with scientific rigidity has come from the study of living things and the evolutionary process, and from the fact that not all agree with the understanding of Darwin. Beginning with the rediscovery of Mendel's laws and a theory of mutations . . . these developments have been as revolutionary as anything in physics. Edwin Schrodinger has remarked that 'the theory of mutations is an atomic theory of heredity. It is for the understanding of the origin of species what the quantum theory is for physics. . . . Jacques Monod has carefully shown the lack of determinism in genetic events. Dr. Charles Mayo has put his finger on the fact that nature does not develop in a smooth and even pattern as Darwin thought, but in jumps and starts. Also, Loren Eiseley shows that the mutation process apparently often prepares for an adaptation rather than the other way around. . . . And Teilhard de Chardin has seen the evolutionary process as an increasing manifestation of spirit, which is always to be found in conjunction with matter. . . . In psychosomatic medicine, it has been discovered that emotions have a real, often very great effect on people's bodily reactions. . . . Dr. Flanders Dunbar assembled evidence from all areas of medicine and showed conclusively that emotional problems often reacted directly on the body. . . . And even more startling, medical men came to realize that even emotions a man does not know he has—unconscious emotions—can disturb and alter bodily functioning" (Kelsey, 1972, p. 100-101).

We leave Kelsey. The evidence is piling much too high and we're losing our perspective on it. Everywhere we turn, if we open our ears, we are hearing a dramatic tale.

We go outside in an effort to get some distance on it. We try to take it slowly but it just rushes over us if we allow ourselves the least openness . . . quantum physics and Einstein's thought . . . potentia, conversion! and talk of God . . . all is relative, even our perception, our feeble and frail mind. The medievals had been in the center of the world but we were removed, no longer sandwiched between heaven and hell. We did a strange thing, however, by denying our inner world, for we, in effect, made ourselves the center of the world. We sealed over the crack to the inner world and then proved its non-existence by our sealing. Our meaninglessnesses, depressions and anxieties, our *angst*, became our focus but how little we admitted this being our center. . . . Oh the center was there, we called it Abyss, and dismissed whatever came from it as illusion, Maya, and dismissed those who actually believed it as deluded primitives. . . . The Indians . . . no delusion there for they healed the sick through the Great Spirit. . . . Oh bosh, rubbish! They just didn't understand the physiology. . . . No? the inner dialogue continues. Well, would you believe our doctors? . . . psychosomatics, and the memory—Hippocrates, Galen, the temples of Asklepios, the use of dreams to heal, and such use healing the doctor considered less than optimal if he denied the dreams. Patients left him for he couldn't heal if the hole was closed. . . . And the hole, perhaps that's the fear, for we hear of the shamans but what of those who were blasted to bits when confronted with this energy, a potential H-bomb of spirituality? . . . But the H-bomb was developed by scientists, some other voice protests . . . and their inspiration came through . . . revelation. . . . Those dancing images when unchanneled can go berserk. No wonder we want nothing to do with them. . . . But if they're channeled, says still another voice, these images can bring healing and creativity. . . . The hole and the Abyss. . . . A narrow bridge connecting the inner and the outer but if you lose your balance, Boom! So hold on and be careful, but walk, Wanderer, walk . . . for it is an incredible world again, one in which images and fantasy can often bring us closer to the truth . . . where reality and unreality are not divided by an Iron Curtain. Walk softly. Have you been watching them, Friedrich? It's now possible to be skeptical of skepticism. Maybe you aren't shouting by yourself now. . . .

Chapter 6 *Psychologists Who Are Looking*

Our mind has considered these new facts to its capability for the moment and our exploring side is itching to move again into action. Turning back to the building we notice an entrance which we hadn't seen before and our curiosity pushes us toward it. We open the door and find the small room empty. But there is evidence of prior furious activity. Papers are strewn about the room; empty coffee cups lie all over the table. On the other side of the room is a door and we open it also. At the end of a dark hallway is the main auditorium where we had been before. Perhaps the workers in this room

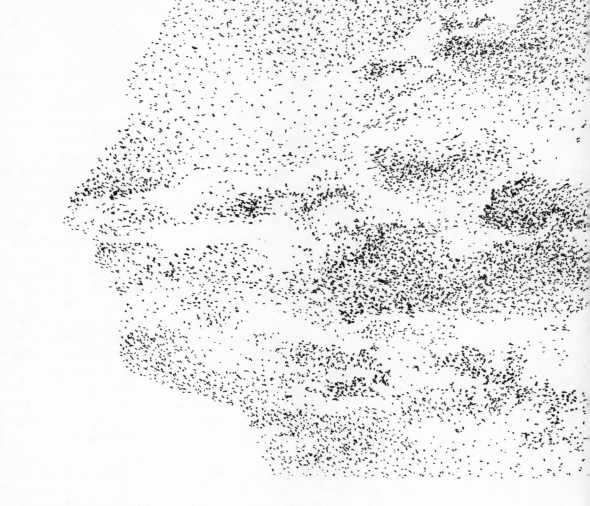

have some important function in the large meeting place.
Perhaps they're doing this important function now. Wondering what it might be, we begin searching around the room and on one of the desks under several books and outlines and papers, we find a hint of the purpose of this room. It is a paper which apparently states the position of the investigators. It reads as follows:

"Psychology, or certain segments of it, has constantly tried to establish itself in the eyes of the 'older' sciences. This hasn't always been easy for, its object of study, the person, seems

ever so much more complex than the objects of physical study, such as electrons, protons, neutrinos. While this point itself may be arguable within some frameworks, the fact remains that most psychology has based itself on what it believed to be the science of the day. Certain disturbing notions appear to some of us, however, when we are reminded, by a physicist of the stature of J. Robert Oppenheimer, that it is futile to model psychological science "after a physics which is not there anymore, which has been quite outdated". For if the physical foundation of our science has eroded and if nineteenth century ideas of causality and materialism and science are inadequate, then as scientists we need to turn elsewhere in our search.

"Disturbing at a much deeper level are the implications which this change to a 'physics which *is* there' has for us. For, in effect, our science disappears in the nuclear reaction. There are parts of our nature which we've deemed impossible which now are demanding reconsideration. The allowance of these parts so changes our view of humanity that it even brings into question the treatment modalities derived from our old views. We are tempted to take Skinner's point of view, so well expressed in *Beyond Freedom and Dignity*: 'The dimensions of the world of mind and the transition from one world to another do raise embarrassing problems, but it is usually possible to ignore them and this may be a good strategy, for the important objection to mentalism is of a very different sort. The world of mind steals the show.' Ignore it, in other words, and it won't cause you much trouble.

"There is, however, a brilliant retort to Skinner, made many years ago by William James who speaks in a different tone about the very same reality. He writes: 'Our normal waking consciousness, rational consciousness as we call it, is but one special type of consciousness, whilst all about it, parted from it by the filmiest of screens, there lie potential forms of consciousness entirely different. We may go through life without suspecting their existence; but apply the requisite stimulus, and at a touch they are there in all their complete-

ness, definite types of mentality which probably somewhere have their field of application and adaptation. No account of the universe in its totality can be final which leaves these other forms of consciousness quite disregarded. . . . They forbid a premature closing of our accounts with reality' (p. 305).

"And so we've heard two important psychologists with radically different approaches to the same data. It reminds us of Jung's work *Psychological Types* in which he shows the importance of personality type in determining what a person will see and experience. Jung's approach is something we will return to momentarily. At present, it is necessary to take a look at the psychological field to see if there are explorers who have heeded Oppenheimer's words. Very soon we find that there are. In the following pages we will examine their findings.

"Perhaps a good way to begin is by standing outside for a moment, looking in, trying to find a way to put what we see together. Thomas Kuhn, working in another part of the building, suggests a starting point when he shows that science works on the basis of shared assumptions of what is possible. These shared assumptions he calls a paradigm. Now a paradigm is, at the same time, limiting and creative. Limiting in that it tells us what is possible and by implication, what is impossible. That which falls in the impossible category cannot be considered within the paradigm. But the paradigm is also creative because it gives us a channel for our facts. It gives us a framework with which to organize the facts. The problem for a paradigm and its followers comes when the paradigm cannot be stretched or remolded to include known facts. The discovery of x-rays, radium, atomic fusion and fission, quantum mechanics, relativity are all modern examples of this overstretching. What happens at these moments of 'no-paradigm' is that scientists are forced back to their philosophical roots and begin to rethink their position so as to allow in the new facts.

"An example or two from our own field will be beneficial here. Jerome Frank reports the use of a stereopticon in an

73

experiment of perception. Subjects were shown simultaneously a picture of a matador and a baseball player, one to each eye. Mexican subjects tended to see the bullfighter while American subjects tended to see the baseball player. In other words, we see what we know while we tend to exclude what we don't know from our vision. Bruner's and Postman's famous study of anomalous cards brings home a similar point. While subjects identified regular playing cards with ease, they 'corrected' the anomalous cards (such as a *red* six of *spades*) to be regular cards (such as a *red* six of *hearts*). Their expectations colored what they saw.

"It is from this perspective that psychology seems to be in line with the modern physical sciences. A number of noted psychologists are studying the effect of paradigm, of expectation, on an individual's awareness. Gardner Murphy speaks of a 'canalization' in which perceptions and ideas are channeled in certain directions and perceptions and ideas which fall outside the channel are ignored or devalued. Arthur Deikman calls this process 'automatization' in which one learns how to react to the world automatically, unconsciously, without questioning the validity of one's assumptions about the world. J. C. Pearce sees a 'cosmic egg' of assumptions in which each of us is enclosed. In George Kelly's framework, each person creates his own world by means of his 'personal constructs' . . . which are similar to scientific hypotheses, and applied to new experiences of the world as long as they work.

"Physiologically too we are limited in what we perceive. Such limitation may be a survival adaptation. In this light, Bergson has suggested that the function of the brain and nervous system is to protect us from being overwhelmed by the tremendous amounts of information which surround us. According to him, the brain is eliminative rather than productive. As an example, consider the fact that only a very small part of the electromagnetic spectrum is visible to us. If this were not so, imagine the 'blooming, buzzing confusion!' of carooming radio waves, alpha waves, x-rays, bouncing about preventing us from sorting anything out. The eliminative function thus serves a creative purpose but it also creates problems. For one thing, our limited sensory systems exclude many forms of energy which cannot fit into the reducing valve. Consider, for example, the difficulty of watching a television program without a tv set. A person from another culture who has never seen a television might think us rather strange if we tried to explain seeing a television program without showing him the tv set. Even then, he will probably have difficulty adjusting to the reality of television.

"A much greater problem may develop (and probably will) within an individual or a culture. The tendency will be to think of one's perception of the world as *the* true one and other perceptions which disagree with it as lacking in truth. Nineteenth century positivism and anthropology had this attitude toward other times and cultures. Both measured other cultures against their own and judged the others inferior in areas of disagreement. Such thinking works from the assumption that one's own perception is the correct one. Is one then to assume that his/her perceptions are incorrect or incomplete? Does the psychologist assume that, in keeping with Heisenberg's Uncertainty Principle and the Bruner-Postman experiment, that his/her perception of the world, of another individual, is colored by his/her own bias, expectations and presence? The answer seems to be yes.

"This allows us to consider the importance of Oppenheimer's remark mentioned above. The psychologist who follows the dictates of a nineteenth century materialistic science will bring different assumptions to his/her meeting with another individual than a psychologist viewing the world from a modern physical perspective. According to our thinking thus far, it is possible that one psychologist will identify a certain experience as a red six of hearts while the other, knowing of the existence of a red six of spades, will see the experience for that. Or using a different image, a psychologist who assumes the existence of the unconscious or of the collective unconscious will react differently to unconscious experiences than will the psychologist who does not assume an unconscious.

"Most important to remember as we examine this area is that we, the psychologists, speak as participants, as interested actors in the drama, rather than as disinterested observers. What we say applies also to ourselves. We too have canalized, automatized, made personal constructs, and surrounded ourselves with a cosmic egg. So in considering the implications of these processes, we will find ourselves affected. Where, one might ask, does this leave us? In several little compartments, little egos, peering through our shells at each other? Is there any way out? Pearce speaks of 'cracking the cosmic egg', Murphy of 'breaking the mold', Deikman of 'deautomatization', Kelly of changing one's personal construct. Each suggests that by doing such we can allow new information into our consciousness; we can establish a new paradigm; we can create a new construct or larger cosmic egg or wider channel for ourselves, the process for each seeming to be a complementary one—the channel and breaking the channel for the 'stuff' of the channel is instrumental in the reestablishment of a new channel. What one already knows goes into the discovery of what one will know. This process is not unlike what happens in science. A paradigm or construct is developed and through work on that construct, new facts emerge which demand the development of a new paradigm from which emerge new facts and so on.

"The processes of individual and of scientific growth thus run parallel courses. 'Psychology' being the 'study of the psyche' is the discipline in which we can view these two growths operating with each other. Let's now take a look at what science can tell us about the individual.

"The first thing to remember is the relativity of our perceptions. We do not expect to find with absolute certainty the ultimate nature of the human individual. What we will find is the perceiver viewing his/her own modes of perception. Here too we will find psychologists who are trying to heed Op-

76

penheimer's reminder.

"Looking inside the head of the individual, the perceiver, we see that grey mattered thinking box, the brain. Perhaps again we remember Skinner's quote and for a moment, mind seems obviously a mere epiphenomenon of the chemical activity of this grey stuff. Nevertheless, even the materialist is interested in looking deeper. Maybe even more interested for this for him is all there is. What we find is that the cerebral cortex is divided into two hemispheres connected by a network of nerves, the corpus callosum. If the corpus callosum is cut, it becomes obvious that the two hemispheres are capable of two quite different modes of thinking. One side, usually the left, is responsible for logical, verbal, analytical thought while the other, usually the right, thinks holistically, synthetically, in images. Nineteenth century science unknowingly valued only one side of the brain. Other cultures, such as the Trobrianders, value the right side but not the left. But there exist also those nerves, the corpus callosum, which would connect the right and the left. It is the corpus callosum which (speaking materialistically but not ontologically) allows scientific and individual psychological growth for these connectors bring about the process we mentioned before (see Ferguson, 1978). First, the verbal logical construct (having to start somewhere) which informs us about the world, about our experiments. Then the image or intuition which suggests a growth beyond the construct to a wider construct and so on. (This is not to forget all those times of difficulty when the growth process has stopped or is reversed.) Perhaps here our left brain protests "that isn't logical.' And this is how we would expect left brain to react for now we have gone beyond its domain. As Roberto Assaglioli states about one of the main activities of the right brain: 'Intuition . . . does not work from the part to the whole—as the analytical does—but apprehends a totality directly in its living existence.' It's understandable why our left brain protests.

"But what of this right brain? How does it manifest itself and how can it be useful to us? Robert Ornstein, one of the leading researchers in this area, has brought together some interesting facts about the right brain, about the holistic side of our brain. The avenue he uses for discussing this holistic approach is the study of traditional Eastern esoteric psychologies such as Yoga, Buddhism, Zen. What these esoteric psychologies do, in essence, according to Ornstein, is to expose one to the realm of timelessness, taking one outside the everyday world of opposites, the 'tonal' as don Juan calls it, into the 'void', the 'abyss', the 'still point', nirvana, satori, samadhi, 'the cosmic ooze' where one transcends Maya, illusion, the absoluteness of one's point of view.

"Meditation is the usual method for attaining this consciousness. As Ornstein tells us, 'Meditation is an attempt to alter consciousness in such a way that other aspects of reality can become accessible to the practitioner.' Meditation reminds us of the red sixes of spades (and the blue twelves of leaves). Through it, one deautomatizes his perception to the point of rearranging it to allow new perception. In the esoteric psychologies, the ultimate is nirvana, satori, the 'cosmic ooze'. And this is a valid goal. The Zen practitioner, in fact, is warned of the dangerous stage of madness, makyo, which is a welter of images that is brought by the devil, a maze in which the adept can be lost forever. This attitude is in keeping with Eastern philosophy's notion that the physical world is illusion or Maya.

There is, however, another possibility, a Western one which should be considered. In this approach, meditation is used to still the inner dialogue as in Eastern meditation but with a different purpose. Instead of seeking nirvana or the transcendence of opposites as a goal, the meditator uses meditation to 'clear the field' so that he/she may relate to the images which arise from the depths. This is a radically different possibility and we need to take a careful look at what is happening in these methods.

"There are at least three ways of doing this. The first view, that verbal, analytical, logical thinking is the only way to knowledge is the normally acceptable Western approach. The second, that besides the verbal there is an ultimate realm of transcendence to be striven for, a void beyond our reasoned world, is the approach of Eastern mysticism and Western adepts to this system. The third view includes the first two but adds that the images of meditation and dreams are important indicators of the direction that the practitioner should pursue and that by denying these images, as do the adherents to the first two views, he/she is sealing off a way to knowledge. It is this third approach, which Jung has called active imagination and which many religious persons have called a form of prayer, which is the closest of the three views to modern science. For the modern physicist does not deny the complementarity of waves of light and particles of light and he doesn't speak of them as merely 'void' or 'nothingness' but as energy from which come the forms, arrangements, perceptions and images of our world.

"What we are suggesting, in essence, is that there exists a realm to which images and dreams introduce us *as well as* a realm of physical sensations and perceptions. About this inner realm we no more reach ultimate certainty through imagery than we do through our outer perceptions of the sensory world. And we must again remember that Principle of Uncertainty as we venture inward for we are affecting the images by our very viewing of them.

"One might counter all this with the argument that if what we say is true there are certainly many people who are ignorant of this inner world. Immediately, we agree with this statement for what we are speaking of is above all a matter of experience. The particular argument is perhaps best stated by Freud and Jung. Freud in *The Future of an Illusion* writes: 'If the truth of religious doctrines is dependent on an inner experience which bears witness to that truth, what is one to do about the many people who do not have this rare experience?' Jung attacks the same problem from the other direction in *Psychology and Religion*. 'I must point out,' he writes 'that there

is no question of belief, but of experience. Religious experience is absolute. It is indisputable. You can only say that you have never had such an experience, and your opponent will say "Sorry, I have." And there your discussion will come to an end.

"Just so. Is this then the end of the argument between outer and inner reality, between left and right brains? And what of the go-between, the corpus callosum, who carries messages (though not always love letters) back and forth between the two? Are we just in the end a house divided against itself? It's possible that these are only partial questions, left brain questions, which are omitting crucial aspects, red sixes of spades (red herrings, some might say), from our answer.

"Let us then turn to our experience and attempt to examine what we know. The first fact which comes to mind is that ever repeating psychological truth about set and setting which proves again and again to be pivotal in the judgments made about experience. It is well known that a person's mental set, his/her attitude toward an experience will affect the experience. (This is still another statement—in positive terms—of the Uncertainty Principle.) If a person expects to have a positive experience (or to experience anything at all), that expectation tends to be self-fulfilling just as a person who expects a negative experience will be more likely to have a negative experience. Setting is equally important for defining one's experience. (Consider the extreme example of the setting of a temple versus the setting of a concentration camp.)

"In essence, set and setting are speaking of the inner and outer conditions of the moment of experience. In the psychological field, there are experimenters who are pointing to the great importance of these factors in the development of our approach to the study of persons. T. X. Barber, for example, has shown that a person's attitudes, motivations and expectations and the experimental setting are such crucial aspects of 'hypnosis' that to postulate a separate 'hypnotic state' may be misleading. In other words, the mental set of the subject and the experimental conditions rather than an imposed state of hypnosis are mainly responsible for the inner experiences of 'hypnotized' subjects in this view. He has gone further to show that subjects who score well while under 'hypnosis' will score as well, or will experience the suggestions as well, when not under hypnosis. Openness to the realm to which 'hypnosis' purportedly admits one can be sufficient entry fee to that realm by itself without undergoing hypnosis. One wonders how much the materialistic attitude of the last few hundred years necessitated the development of an outer method which allowed for and explained inner experience. One could always say afterwards, 'Well, it happened because I was hypnotized' as if that explains anything.

"Still another area, one whose understanding has tremendous cultural import, is the use of psycho-active drugs. The question asked often by distraught parents and by many drug-takers themselves is 'Why? What need have they (we) for drugs, for freaking out, for acid trips?' It is a good question—depending on what one is really asking. For many, the question speaks of despair and fear, the crumbling of old values. For others, however, there is a slight twist; they see something important happening which must be understood.

"Using the present framework, an explanation would go something like this: Individuals are running away from lives which are meaningless, some in search of meaning, some merely to escape. In a society which generally refuses the reality of an inner spiritual world or a right-brained world there are several options. One is to accept the meaninglessness stoically as the individual watches the mechanical universe grind inexorably on. Another is to despair of the culture altogether and turn to the East in search of 'cosmic bliss'. Still another is to give oneself to a fundamental religious group, receiving salvation on a platter once and for all. Another popular route is to seek escape or meaning through drugs in an attempt to awaken one's dormant impossible inner nature. Psychologists see the results of this route all too often, for many lose their way, captured in the cave of makyo, and wander aimlessly through the labyrinth of images. They are naked, unprepared, without a framework which can make their experience meaningful.

"Part of the problem, then, is the mental set and the setting of the experiencer. Most experiencers stumble upon a world which has been dead and impossible for many generations—at least in any immanent sense, for either God has died or He sits in moral judgment on some fluffy cloud up there. And thus disconnected, they are zapped by an Almighty Impossible.

"Someone might argue here that we're neglecting the Huxleys and Watts and the peyote cultists who have postulated and experienced meaning through mescaline, LSD, MDA, and other psychotropic agents. In our opinion, the mistake that they are making is a crucial one. As Andrew Weil notes in *The Natural Mind*, highs come from inner conditions rather than from an outer agent. What psychotropic drugs do is to open the taker to a realm of himself which he does not presently know how to enter otherwise. It is worth noting that among other cultures, especially primitive tribal ones, it is still possible to enter this inner realm and have a similar experience without using drugs. And as Aniela Jaffe tells us in *The Myth of Meaning*: 'An artificially induced experience of the unconscious does not as a rule accord with the development and maturity of the personality. This discrepancy harbors a danger . . .'" Taken together, Weil and Jaffe are warning us that drugs are a danger because they put us in *inner* touch with a deeper reality in a way which may be inconsistent with, and dangerous for, our level of personality development.

"But all this still doesn't tell us how to proceed. So they shouldn't do it, still they do. This approach isn't helping at all. What is the next step? On the one hand, they should be provided with a framework which can at least give them a chance to grapple with these inner realities. On the other, we need to provide meaningful alternatives, the most obvious one in our mind being meditation, in which they can meet the inner figures with their own juices, head-on. It is largely for this reason, perhaps, that the major religions have developed. Communal support and spiritual direction was provided to the initiate who made his/her journey. And as with outer reality, the initiate needed this guidance to help him through dangerous territory.

"This brings to mind still another area of the terrain; perhaps for many the most despised and most threatening. Words such as extrasensory perception, precognition, clairvoyance, psychokinesis, telepathy, mediumship, discarnate personalities, out-of-body experiences and psychic healing are heard again and again. We read in an article in *The New York Times* that about forty percent of persons interviewed claimed to have had mystical experiences. We see money being spent for experimentation on, of all things, dream telepathy, and with positive results! And others who purportedly can bend forks mentally or know facts physically impossible for them to know. And strange dreams of the death or injury of loved ones which turn out to be prophetic. Even stranger looking into a Western religious text, the New Testament, we find nearly fifty percent of its passages dealing with visions, prophetic dreams, healings.

"Perhaps it is these healings which most upset and enthrall us for even today we hear numerous reports of healing, many of which prove to be false but there are those few. . . . One way that many of these healers work is by meditating and then forming an image of the patient as well or whole, and it reportedly often works, given the faith of the patient. Such results put the skeptic in the position of preferring rational explanations to wholeness or healing and this belies his/her attitude about what is possible in the world (see, e.g., Panati, 1974, LeShan, 1973, Carlson, 1975).

"We shouldn't be too hard on the skeptic, however, given the long history of denying the possibility of non-materialistic healing. And think of the incredible philosophical demands that it makes on him/her. For not only does one have to hypothesize a nonmaterial realm; one must also allow that realm to have an effect on the material world.

"This recalls that important physiological bridge, the corpus callosum. While the two hemispheres are organs and symbols of two aspects of reality, the corpus callosum is the organ and symbol of integration. It is the reminder to each hemisphere that it is not sufficient in itself but a servant to the process of greater wholeness. Each side speaks its truth but needs the other to complete it. We need the spark as much as we need our reason if we are to grow.

"And again, for the individual the process of growth is similar to the process of growth in science. Why then the discrepancy among individual experiences and attitudes? This is the important question, the one which continues the argument, the one which makes both attitudes necessary. For Freud the non-experiencer is right to raise his objections to religious experience (for example) as Jung the experiencer is right to speak for religious experience.

"Remembering that mental set and setting are such crucial factors in experience, we are led to wonder about the origins of a person's mental set. (Setting is pretty clear to us Westerners, although perhaps too clear.) Oppenheimer's warning recalls Heisenberg's Uncertainty Principle. To know the experience we must know the experiencer. What if certain experiencers have an innate advantage over others in experiencing the inner world? What if the others have a corresponding advantage in the perception of the outer world? On a cultural level, language would then be the 'corpus callosum' working between them, forcing each to acknowledge that he/she is experiencing only a part of reality. On a personal level, we could then begin an exploration of psychological types which brings us back to Jung who wrote a book of that name. In this early book, Jung lay the foundation for all his later. . . ."

And that's it! Searching through the papers and through the file cabinets we cannot find out what the author went on to say, if the author has continued. This may be where the project rests. But our impatience has the better of us now. On the bookshelf in the corner we see a large black volume on the binding of which *Psychological Types*, Volume 6, Collected Works of C. G. Jung is written. There's no telling when, or if, the author will return so we settle into an old stuffed chair and begin to read, to find out for ourselves.

Chapter 7   *Jung's View of the Landscape*

Psychological Types turns out to be an enormous book in more than size. A plethora of ideas have come to us while reading it although it will only be possible here to consider it in light of our journey and purpose. Still, the book itself is there for other explorers and others have looked at it from different perspectives, notably von Franz and Hillman (1971).

At the outset, it would be wise to note that Jung wrote this book while in his forties after his own arduous and frightening confrontation with the unconscious. What he speaks of possesses experiential reality for him. In essence, he develops a

framework for the experiences reported by don Juan, the Indian medicine men, the shamans, our Western historical relatives, the physical scientists and the psychologists. He suggests the possibility of understanding our journey in a dynamic way.

Jung certainly isn't the first to attempt to understand the psychological differences among individuals and the incredible difficulties and catastrophies that these differences can cause. Nor does he claim any final statement on this problem. Indeed, he sees it as an historical issue which goes far back into antiquity. At the very beginning he quotes Heine: "Plato and Aristotle! These are not merely two systems, they are types of two distinct human natures, which from time immemorial, under every sort of disguises, stand more or less inimically opposed. The whole medieval world in particular was riven by this conflict, which persists down to the present day, and which forms the most essential content of the history of the Christian Church. Although under other names, it is always of Plato and Aristotle that we speak. Visionary, mystical, Platonic natures disclose Christian ideas and the corresponding symbols from the fathomless depths of their souls. Practical, orderly Aristotelian natures build out of these ideas and symbols a fixed system, a dogma and a cult. Finally the Church embraces both natures, one of them entrenched in the clergy and the other in monasticism, but both keeping up a constant feud."

While Jung goes on to tell this history, it is our purpose to examine the feud. We will refer to the history here only to enlighten our understanding of the feud.

Two distinct human natures. It's an incredible idea although it too easily can become a we/they battle, we of course being the good guys, they the bad. "It is more than probable," Jung writes, "that the contrast of types will also be found in the history of schisms and heresies that were so frequent in the disputes of the early Church" (p. 20).

Depending on which "distinct human nature" you might align yourself with, the good guys and bad guys might be either the establishment or the heretics for you. It is certainly arguable that an establishment nature might tend to be more secure and comfortable than a heretical one. This probably explains in part why the heretics were fewer in number.

But what makes the difference? Is it religious preference? But then what are the factors which make one stance preferable to another for a person? Maybe one's psychological make-up? If so, then we need to elaborate these factors. Jung tells us that he has "found from experience that the basic psychological functions, that is, functions which are genuinely as well as essentially different from other functions, prove to be *thinking*, *feeling*, *sensation*, and *intuition*. If one of these functions habitually predominates, a corresponding type results . . . *Each of these types may moreover be either extraverted or introverted*, depending on its relation to the object" (p. 6).

Thinking, according to Jung (p. 481) "should . . . be confined to the linking up of ideas by means of a concept, in other words, to an act of judgment. . . ." "Feeling is primarily a process that takes place between the *ego* . . . and a given content . . . that imparts to the content a definite *value* in the sense of acceptance or rejection" (p. 434). These two are the judgmental functions and are considered opposites, because one cannot use both forms of judgment at the same time.

"Sensation is the psychological function that mediates the perception of a physical stimulus . . . [it] is related not only to external stimuli but to inner ones" (p. 461). Intuition ". . . is the function that mediates perception in an *unconscious way*. . . . In intuition, a content presents itself whole and complete, without our being able to explain or discover how this content came into existence" (p. 453). These two are the perceptive functions and are considered opposites, again because one cannot perceive in both ways at the same time.

Introversion and extraversion are two attitudes whose distinction is based on the individual's attitude toward the object. "Extraversion is an outward-turning of *libido* . . . Everyone in the extraverted state thinks, feels, and acts in relation to the object . . . so that no doubt can remain about his positive dependence on the object" (p. 427). "Introversion means an inward turning of *libido* . . . in the sense of a negative relation of subject to object. The subject is the prime motivating factor" (452).

Everyone, to some degree, uses all four functions and both attitudes. One speaks of a type, as Jung told us, when one function habitually predominates; e.g., the thinker whose behavior and thoughts are habitaully based on logical decisions.

When one function is preferred, it is developed while the other functions are not so well developed. The problem of differences in perception and judgment in different personality types becomes obvious. As Jung writes (p. 99): "Only one part of the world . . . can be grasped by thinking, another part by feeling, a third only by sensation and so on. That is probably why there are different psychic functions; for, biologically, the psychic system can be understood only as a system of adaptation, just as the eyes exist presumably because there is light." According to this viewpoint, different types are experiencing different parts of reality, or are experiencing reality differently. The reason for the feud between individuals can now be seen more clearly. As an example, an introverted intuitive who explains and understands the world through unconscious inner perceptions will have great difficulty conveying this point of view in a convincing way to an extraverted sensation type. In extreme forms, they have little common ground for discussion.

And worse than two distinct human natures, we have now at least eight distinct natures, each with its own views, perceptions and judgments about the world, each as correct as the other in that each type is merely reporting on its own experience. Jung tells us that the man who puts his own primary function on a pinnacle and who finds the opposite function antipathetic to his personality, "can be compared to a man who has good eyes but is totally deaf and suffers from anaesthesia" (p. 100).

Maybe neither the heretic nor the establishmentarian was totally wrong. Maybe each was viewing a part of reality and considering that part the whole of reality. This is reminiscent of what we found earlier concerning our two brains, the left and right hemispheres. In fact, these two brains seem to have been arguing throughout history. This can be seen in the feud between the nominalists and the realists. The nominalists [left thinkers] "asserted that so-called universals . . . such as beauty, goodness, animal, man, etc. are nothing but *nomina*, names or words . . . Realism [right thinking] affirms the existence of universals *ante rem* and holds that general concepts exist in themselves after the manner of Platonic ideas" (Jung, p. 26). Each considers his point of view the correct one and denies the value of the other point of view.

This is done for good psychological reasons, however. For the first project of the individual is to develop a function for dealing with and organizing the world. But while the individual becomes more habituated to viewing the world through one of the functions (thinking, feeling, sensation, intuition), the other functions are ignored and left undeveloped to a greater or lesser degree. Particularly that function which is the opposite of the favorite function (e.g. feeling for the thinker) will be undeveloped.

Now imagine the feud potential between the thinker who has totally ignored his feeling and the feeling type that has ignored his thinking. All that is valuable and that explains the world to one is devalued and says nothing of the world to the other. Here we have arrived at the dilemma. The individual needs to develop a particular function for his/her orientation to the world, but that same individual excludes much of the world in that same development.

What then is the resolution? Does the feud just continue, and we say we're sorry, but at least now we understand? Does a Stoic attitude allow us to be patient with the differences, despairing of ever changing them? That's one possibility. Another is to take the second step which Jung calls the sacrifice, the giving up, of the primary function. This second step presumes the first, i..e, the development of one's primary function and orientation to the world. When one sacrifices one's primary function, when one closes one's eyes for a moment, then that individual opens him/herself to the opportunity of hearing more fully, of experiencing a part of the world which one normally filters out.

As with Kuhn's anomalies, this can be a very painful process because now one is trying to fit new perceptions into an old framework which may not hold them. The thinker, for instance, who withholds his thinking judgments may become enmeshed in a world of incredible fantastic feelings. Or the intuitive by withholding his hunches may instead find himself in an amazing, frightening world of sensation, as sensory experience which his intuition normally blocked out rushes over him. The same goes for the feeling and the sensation types. And perhaps each will wonder how the opposite types can bear this "bloomin' buzzin' confusion!" The answer is, quite simply, they don't. The habitualized developed sensation of the sensation type greatly differs from the undeveloped sensation of the intuitive.

It seems quite a sacrifice indeed to give up one's primary orientation for one is confronted with the greater world, the world perhaps of the shamans and medicine men. The sacrificial process is akin to the initiatory rite in which the youth gives up his boyhood attitude to become a man. This then is the purpose of the sacrifice, to let the old standpoint die so that a new one can be born.

But what new attitude do we speak of? This disjointed bewilderment? Yes, that but with a twist. For there is a third step beyond developing an initial orientation and its sacrifice. This third step is our creative relation to these opposites so that another, a more whole, attitude can develop which incorporates them. But "opposites are not to be united rationally. . . ." Jung tells us. "That is precisely why they are called opposites . . . In practice, opposites can be united only in the form of a compromise, or *irrationally*, some new thing arising between them which, although different from both, yet has the power to take up their energies in equal measure as an expression of both and of neither. Such an expression cannot be contrived by reason, it can only be created through living . . ." through "a symbol in which the opposites are united" (p. 105).

The existence of the symbol assumes a symbol producing function which Jung calls the transcendent function. It is through this that the individual of whatever type can transcend his/her old orientation in a way which allows the admittance of previously unacceptable experience. While this probably won't stop the feud outside the individual it will begin to solve the inner feud.

In this thinking is the kernel of Jung's technique of active imagination. The transcendent function which makes active imagination a meaningful process works much as a "corpus callosum", acknowledging both realities and uniting them in a greater whole. It is through fantasy, through active imagination, that we come into creative contact with the archetypal world, the world of images and dreams.

But at this the feud strikes up again. Some part of our mind protests. It is the extraverted sensation side, the culturally acceptable side, which is watching from without for it cannot see the world in this way. Remember, it says, Jung speaks from *his* point of view. What he says has no final validity. All right, we answer, but the same applies to you. Jung agrees: "It is a fact . . . that people are virtually incapable of understanding and accepting any point of view other than their own. . . . Every man is so imprisoned in his own type that he is simply incapable of fully understanding another standpoint" (p. 489).

If this is so, then the appropriate attitude for understanding oneself and the world of others is through humility for there are simply no final conclusions, no final certainties. Jung writes: "The type problem must, to say the least of it, be a very unwelcome obstacle for every theory of complex psychic processes that lays claim to general validity (p. 490). . . . Should, therefore, the existence of typical differences of human psyches be granted—and I confess that I see no reason why it should not be granted—the scientific theorist is confronted with the disagreeable dilemma of either allowing several contradictory theories of the same process to exist side by side, or of making an attempt . . . to found a sect which claims for itself the only correct method and the only true theory" (pp. 493-494).

93

So Jung's answer to the feud is that the feud continues. One must not expect to stop it but he can at least see his own part and by sacrificing the absoluteness of his point of view open himself to other aspects of reality. Jung has shown that *conscious* living opens the individual to greater possibilities of growth and wholeness.

So far we've come a long way on our journey. Our attitude has been challenged time and time again. We've heard of the terrible and beautiful worlds within and without, of seeing and using these worlds, of opening our minds to greater possibilities, of our own contribution to what we experience. Now we stop for we have come to a tunnel. The path leads underground; it is time to look within.

PART TWO

Chapter 8 *Looking Within—A New Journey*

Entering the tunnel, we find ourselves surrounded by darkness for the natural light of the sun cannot reach us here. All at once, what has gone before shifts itself and we are confused about what it can all mean, about how we are to put it all together. There is no final certainty, of that we are (paradoxically) certain. It has become clear that our culture, our time, our physiological make-up, our viewpoint and our psychological type all limit us, focus us on a particular world which we take for the world as it is. The paradox of the certainty of uncertainty, what Socrates calls the knowledge of one's igno-

rance, becomes oppressive in this closed, dark, and probably dangerous tunnel.

We sit in the darkness for awhile, hoping for some magical reintegration of what we have experienced into a coherent whole. We would even be satisfied with some solid rule of complementarity here in the darkness for the feud seems meaningless, of the so-what variety, as we sit.

Then a painful process begins. In the dark, in this lonely cavern, our skin begins to shed. Our (my) old rotting covering becomes dust and falls away from us (me). We (I) are (am) no

longer able to identify with our (my) dead skin. Part of the
dead skin, getting near the painfully delicate new covering, is
the we-attitude but, as with the rest, its rotting is beyond me
(us) and with a final slight tear, I am free of it.

It seems ever so much darker now for 'We' has gone and I
am left alone. With We's departure, I am frightened and the
journey seems no more than a trick. (A trick! You win, don
Juan!) For We provided me with some company, supported
me, stood with me and watched. But We has gone or waits
among the dust which surrounds me. We becomes Other, a
company sufficient without me.

I sink with myself into the darkness which mirrors my own
inner darkness and for a timeless moment, darkness is all there
is. Free from the light of the sun, in the dark ooze, even I
threatens to dissolve, to fall from. . . . Now the air isn't, even
the dark isn't, the Mind shrinks in a coldness that isn't, grows
into itself, an incredible black hole of non-life which would
swallow a Universe that isn't. . . . But what! a spark . . . the
hole . . . isn't—it a hole to SomethingOneWhere? "Don't you
have now the chance in this darkness to see your own world,
the stuff of you which helps make the world around you?"
says a voice.

Suddenly, a welter of images. Makyo. Zen madness. The
world of the devil.

Heisenberg's Uncertainty Principle. The observer affects
the experience.

Don Juan's nagual, the fractured tonal unable to repress the
witnessing of the terrible and beautiful world.

The shamanic medicinal hole through which bursts healing
not unlike the journey of the new baby.

History's shouts and whimpers, as some are burned while
the fire goes out in the spirit of others . . . and is rekindled
there or somewhere else.

Constructs, eggs, and channels . . . the Brain making smaller so the world can fit its circuitry. Neurons, thought-
containers, jumping across the Bridge of Corpus Callosum,

trying to ignite what would be darkness.

And a little voice in the midst of it all, whispering through the clamoring makyo.

"But who are you? In all this noise, who are you?"

Who am I? Why a skinshedding journeyman at least.

"Who are you?" says the voice a little louder.

Well then, an individual who's trying to balance all the uncertainty.

"Who?" in a voice now a Whirlwind of makyo-containing Power.

Who? we wonder.

Who?

Not we but I.

Surrounded by a fathomless silence, perhaps now at the eye of the Whirlwind, enclosed in it, the answer is obvious.

I don't know.

"Then you had better begin to remember and let the remembering teach you," says the voice again in a whisper.

I am alone, again in the tunnel, in the darkness, but there is now a glimmering, a remembered spark. Something in me is ready, though afraid of another shedding, with its answer. I can only give myself to it in this tunnel, only listen as it flows forth. . . .

"As you've grown, the Ego, the I, has grown with you. It has become strong and stronger until it began to feel itself the whole world. It forgot the Whirlwind. That is all right and necessary. It has been a preparation for the next stage. This, you and many other little Egos have been preparing for, sometimes without even knowing it. What you and the other Egos must do is to interact with each other and let your individual I's teach each other. This way you can show each other the greater world beyond your constructs. Then you must take that information within and let the deeper world expand you so that you can again go outside and present what your I has discovered. This is desperately important and I need you and the other I's to make your separate statements which together

99

express the fullness. For each ego is itself a corpus callosum, a connector of the worlds of analysis and synthesis, reason and myth, science and religion."

There now is the initial question about science and religion. The answer suggests an inner confrontation and an inner working together—with Ego, I, as the empiricist, as the experiencer, and as part of the object of exploration—both Kant's subject-in-itself and object-in-itself.

This stops me. (I want to say this stops *us*.) I, the subject, must be an object of my own study (and of others' study as I interact with them). This demands a statement of who I am and an examination of how that statement affects my stand in the world. It isn't easy, for the visible parts don't blend comfortably or Ego doesn't know how to blend them. Each side seems to fear the rejection of the other. But though that's true, I cannot let it stop me if I wish to continue my journey.

It goes like this. I am committed to psychology and to Christianity, and sometimes to Christian psychology. This is where I am though it seems strangely embarrassing. Perhaps I feel like some atavism, some throwback to a pre-modern time. But that is the thinking of nineteenth century positivism and naturalism—and it is just this thinking which is atavistic. Perhaps instead I am an anomaly, a red six of spades, which needs to be incorporated or at least scrutinized before the card game continues.

Christian psychology. Analysis splits them neatly into two—Christian and psychology; Christian representing a right-brain stance, psychology a left-brain stance. Putting the two together is the work of the corpus callosum, the I. Nonetheless, if I or any other Ego or individual is to be understood, if the individual anomaly is to be incorporated, then analysis is necessary. For along with the whole, the separate parts must be seen in themselves.

In my case, in this particular instance, I'm speaking of two categories which are much broader than myself and indeed are much different realities for different members of each group of

Christians and psychologists. Immediately, this being my particular journey, I remember personality types, though this in itself is not an explanation but rather a framework within which to search for explanations. At this point, personality type only reminds me of the need for humility in my statements about the "essence" of Christianity and psychology. It also makes me aware of other types who will (or may) totally disagree with my formulation and of my innate response which tries to convert them to my view.

With this in mind, I realize at once that a consideration of the "two worlds" of Christianity and psychology seems in line with what that voice said to me earlier; the ego is a connector between two worlds. For the moment, we (you and I) will be looking beyond the ego to the wider realities. In other words, with this attitude, ego can be transcended quite easily, so that we may consider what is interesting and meaningful for both of us.

It may seem presumptuous to tackle these two large realities. It seems so to me but, keeping in mind the relativity of the statements and their lack of any final validity, I can proceed, speaking as an experiencer rather than as an expert. And further, this presumptuous tackling is what we do daily as we make our different ways in the world.

First of all, Christianity. Being a Christian is, of course, only one of many possible religious professions. Judaism, Islam, Hinduism, Buddhism, Sufism, Jainism, all these are possibilities. And there are many others. Christianity then can be understood as one of many possible formulations of deeper reality, of the world of myth and dream and symbol, of ESP and other non-rational experiences. Each formulation imposes on reality its own values and one who professes a faith acknowledges that his or her formulation seems best to fit his or her experience of reality. But from Heisenberg and from Weil, we know that the observer affects the world which he views. One who views the world through the Christian experience thus affects it differently than, for instance, the Buddhist. It is not for the Christian (or Buddhist or atheist) to 'prove' rationally that his or her experience is superior to another's experience. It is rather the Christian's (or Buddhist's or atheist's) obligation to report the experiences of that approach to life, making it available for others to discover which is most meaningful for himself or herself.

This would be very nice and tidy, were it not for the fact that Christianity (and Buddhism and atheism) is further divided into sects which define reality and the means to experience it at its deepest in different ways. Historical trends further muddy the waters. For being a Christian before and after the victory of Constantine, for example, meant radically different things to the professor. Before, one was the persecuted who needed to be very committed to face the jaws of the lion joyfully. After Constantine, Christianity became the official state religion opening the door for the less committed and in later years forcing some of the committed out of the fold. Again, history makes the experience often very different. The early Christians spoke of the experience of visions of the Risen Christ, which pronouncement makes many of us moderns blush and cover over their tracks. For naturalism and positivism have convinced us of the impossibility of such events really occurring; this to the point where the leading theologians spend a good bit of their energy "demythologizing" (Bultmann) or "dispensationalizing" (Barth) the experiences of the Bible and the new Christians. It either, these arguments go, didn't happen that way or God dispensed with natural law for the moment and afterwards reinstituted natural law.

But all this slides us safely away from the experience, keeping us in our left brain if you will. The theologians fell for the argument of positivism even though they put themselves in a laughable position by so doing, writing reams and reams showing that the experience really wasn't anything special. It could be argued, as in Chapter 6, that those who presently feel the need for deep experience are forced to go to the East or to drugs while leaving something of value behind, something hidden from them which may be very different from the Eastern or drug experiences of the depths.

Oppenheimer's warning now comes to mind. The world of physics is radically different from what it was and we mustn't base our psychology on a physics which isn't there anymore. But I'm talking here about religion not psychology. Perhaps it's psychology which has made the connection, for modern religion often seems to have given up its calling. It is psychology which has begun to listen to Oppenheimer and the other physicists, those psychologists who are reopening our thinking to the "anomaly" of religious experience.

In a way, we have left historical religious experience only to return to it through psychology. We should turn to psychology for a moment to understand its import for modern religion. But here a familiar problem again appears. Psychology, as we've seen with religion, has taken many paths and in so doing has arrived at many viewpoints about the nature of the human individual. From one psychological perspective, this is seen as a result of psychological type, many explanations being rendered for the many different experiences of reality by individuals of these different types. But here again a theory of psychological type provides a framework for understanding rather than an understanding itself. Further steps are needed to approach such an understanding.

Beyond that, psychological type is of no consequence devoid of experience. While the given type may limit or define to a great degree what the experience means, it is not the sole cause of what experience comes to the individual. To make typology the sole determinant of experience would be a form of solipsism, denying the reality of an objective world beyond the individual. It could be argued that such an approach would be due to a complete surrender to one's own type which essentially denies the experience of those types who place their value primarily on the objective rather than subjective reality.

This leads us to consider the experience of the individual along with typology. Finding one's way on one's own particular path is the important issue. In the present case, the journey on which you've come with me, we've heard of don Juan's terrible and beautiful world, watched the healing relation to the Spirit of the Indian medicine men and the shamans, glimpsed the search for knowledge through Western history, seen the radical upheaval in the physical sciences and the radical following in psychology and finally read Jung's ideas about why the unfolding of all these processes is a bit messier than the progressivism imagined by thinkers of the Enlightenment.

For the moment, let's place type on the backburner and reflect on this experience from a particular psychological perspective. We must again remark that, depending on one's psychological viewpoint, these experiences can be construed in many different ways. What is important to us, our particular bias, is to weigh as much as possible the merits of each experience without at the same time losing our own point of view. For this, we need a psychological perspective which sees the values inherent in the experiences of each stop of our journey. At once, it is obvious (remember that type is on the backburner, not discarded) that a positivistic psychology which denies most of the experiences outright or labels them as "nothing-but" experiences will not allow us to consider these experiences on their own merit. The judgment will have already been made about their worthlessness or superstitious quality. Let me say that the positivist psychologist can make different observations regarding this or his own journey but his observations will seem less than optimal to this journeyman for they will fail to consider all the facts. As I write these words I feel myself to be one of the combatants in the ongoing feud. That is as it is.

Beyond this, however, there does exist a psychology which attempts to take these many experiences into account. Not surprisingly, given the unfolding of the journey, this is the analytical psychology proposed by Jung. He found, in work with modern patients from all over the world, an inner reality which is much like that described by don Juan. A diagram

(Kelsey, 1972, p. 111) may serve us as a roadmap for viewing this terrain:

Non-Space-Time World   Space-Time World

The Self   destructive   Psyche
              tendencies

A   A   A   A

A-Archetypes

Jung sees the world divided into two realities, two types of experience: first, the outer, everyday space-time world of normal experience and also the inner non-space-time world of dreams, visions, religious experience, psi experiences and so on. Psyche, or Ego, is the percipient who lives in both worlds. This view of the world is not unlike don Juan's division of the world into the tonal (our everyday experiences) and the nagual (that of which we are unaware which emerges through "jolts"). Jung's archetypes are configurations of energy or power which appear again and again in the dreams and myths and visions of humanity. These same experiences are seen in the allies of don Juan. For both men, the individual's attitude determines whether his or her relationship to the archetypes or allies is creative or destructive. The Self, for Jung, is the transcending principle which influences and provides meaning for the individual but is more than Psyche. It is the source from which comes all life. For don Juan, power is the source of all things in the world. An important distinction between the two men is that while don Juan sees the nagual or the inner world as something to be witnessed, Jung goes further and sees the inner world as providing meaning and as capable of bringing healing. His position is much closer to the medicine men and shamans who served as mediators between their tribes and the Great Spirit, or Wakan Tanka. The Indians, shamans and Jung all see a negative powerful force existing in the world, a reality, which could make people sick and even kill them. Their job as psychologist, doctor or shaman is to bring the stricken individual into creative relationship with the Great Spirit, the Healer, the Self. For them, the inner world, beyond being witnessed, is an incredibly powerful reality to which individuals could and must relate creatively and through which they obtain health and wholeness. The inner world is, in other words, a world to be reckoned with in everyday life. By denying it or by relating to it incorrectly one became potentially more open to illness and even death.

At this, don Juan reminds us that death must be our best friend, that it is with death we have our inevitable last dance and this is something to be reckoned with. It is however, a pervasive problem which can be considered fully only at the end of this consideration of the journey from Jung's perspective.

We are now confronted with our speedy jaunt through Western history. Jung's theory of types (while remembering the particular experiences of the individuals and the historical settings) gives us a glimpse of what has been going on throughout history. To put it in general terms, while the two realities have existed throughout time, individuals and societies have been selective about which aspects of reality to value in those places and times. When one aspect of reality became overly valued to the neglect of another, a representative(s) of the type which valued the neglected aspect was likely to speak for that aspect in an attempt (often unconscious) to bring about a balance between the two aspects. In our own time and culture, for example, there are many who are attempting to renew the value of the inner world. Some like don Juan would have us "simply" witness this world while others are open to the possibility of a meaningful relationship to this inner world. All of this is not to say that there hasn't existed an undercurrent of "inner-worldliness". It only states that the "inner-world" hasn't been generally valued by our society, much as in India, the outer world isn't valued.

This psychological perspective also is in line with modern physics, perhaps especially with the theories of relativity, complementarity and quantum mechanics. The notion of two worlds which must be considered in Jung's psychology for a whole picture is much like Bohr's theory of complementarity, the need for explaining light sometimes as waves and sometimes as particles while either explanation in itself is incomplete. Jung's theory of types is also directly related to Einstein's theories of relativity and Heisenberg's Principle of Uncertainty. We experience the world relative to our type and relative to where we are in the world. And we can never be certain about the essential nature of what we see or experience because we, as subject, affect it.

Modern psychosomatic medicine which sees much disease as stress related, and which sees the emotions, the inner world and the attitude of the individual as terribly important for health, also is in line with the thinking of both Jung and the medicine men and shamans. One psychiatist, Jerome Frank, even sees faith in some instances as being as effective in healing as is penicillin in other cases. Modern evolutionary theories which postulate a purpose and meaning behind evolution also can be accepted as possible within this psychological perspective.

The last outer stop in our journey, with the psychologists, indicates that much experimentation is being done with altered states of consciousness, with suggestibility, with ESP, and with the two hemispheres of the brain which can be understood in the Jungian framework. By positing a nonphysical world through which these experiences can come, and with the possibility of the experiences being meaningful, the value of this research is greatly enhanced.

107

Jung, then, provides a useful framework for understanding our journey thus far. But here we must remember that our very last encounter on our journey has been with the inner world, with ourselves, with you and me. Jung's perspective has helped us evaluate that which we have found outside of us, but can this perspective be as valuable within?

Remember that in this particular case, we are speaking of Christian psychology. The obvious question which comes to mind is, how does Christian psychology fit in here? For though we have seen the value of a religious approach to reality, the Christian approach hasn't been singled out as particularly useful.

On a practical level, this is important since we are speaking of Christianity and not Buddhism, Islam or Sufism. The percipient, or ego, here professes a Christian view and from our journey we know that one's viewpoint is an all important consideration concerning what one will experience.

Well then, what is this Christian understanding? And why Christianity rather than, say, Buddhism or atheism? These are two enormous questions not lightly dealt with and crucial to our understanding. It might be said that half of our experience, that of our right hemisphere, is at stake. And further, remembering the corpus callosum, that all experience, inner and outer, are affected by it for the inner changes the outer as well as vice versa.

And so, Christianity. It shouldn't be too difficult. Christianity is the result of the life of one historical personage, Jesus of Nazareth, and of the institution which has developed through twenty centuries after him. Jesus claimed to be the Saviour; the Church claims to represent his message and make him a living, viable presence today.

Such a host of retorts rushes in that it's difficult to know where to begin. First, a quick saying of some of them. To speak of "the Church" seems a bit out of focus for the Church is not one but many churches and with many different viewpoints, often contrary to one another in their understanding of Jesus' life and of "the Church's" mission. There are, for instance, the Catholics, Anglicans, Methodists, Baptists, Quakers, Congregationalists, Unitarians, Lutherans and factions within each. There are fundamentalists who profess immediate salvation and form critics who speak of the New Testament as a myth, as a formula for describing what happened in Jesus' life in a dramatic but essentially untrue way. Perhaps in some way, there's again a problem of type here—at least in the original formulations of these sects.

This then leads us to another retort. What of this man Jesus and his experiences? Nearly half of the verses about him and his followers in the New Testament deal with supernatural happenings, with healings, dreams and visions, with raising people from the dead, with voices from heaven and angels and devils and Satan. But much of this makes more sense if we allow our right brain to be involved and if we consider with Jung the reality of an inner world of power capable of healing and of bringing meaning through dreams and visions. Perhaps we do best here to recall our diagram and to "Christianize" it. It would then look like this:

Spiritual World   Temporal World

God, Jesus, Holy Spirit

Angels,   Angels,   Angels,   Angels,
Demons   Demons   Demons   Demons

Psyche   The Evil
or   One,
Soul   Satan

Remember that you and I are dealing with a particular percipient, trying to understand that percipient's view of the world. In this diagram, the experiential world is "spiritualized". As with Jung, the psychologist viewed the world in nonreligious terms. Here the percipient views the same reality in spiritual terms.

But is it then the same reality? If so, then what difference do the terms make? The Christian percipient would say that the terms do make a difference. Let's look at what the supposed difference is. First of all, the Christian has personalized the diagram to a great degree by seeing Jesus as a flesh and blood manifestation of the Great Spirit, of Wakan Tanka, who as such took on our humanity, participating in it to the full, to the pits of a gruesome agony and a bloody humiliating death. And more, if one reads the whole account, he supposedly rose from the dead. This of course seems incredibly ridiculous to the scientific mind—or half-mind one might say. For myths from all over the world have proclaimed a dying and rising God and the myth of rebirth was celebrated every spring by many peoples. There are, for example, the myths of Adonis and Aphrodite, Tammuz and Ishtar, Attis and Cybele, Osiris and Isis. If one takes myth seriously, as an imaginative statement of the right brain, one suspects the possibility of a reality being spoken of in these myths. And a people like the Israelites place(d) all their hope in the coming of a Messiah. There is, in other words, a deep longing in human beings for rebirth of the spiritual nature and of a conquering of death. Kelsey (1974) tells of the dying/rebirth cults that arose around both Lincoln and Kennedy after their assassinations. Within our culture too, there still remains this same hope and longing. But it is hard to hope too much, to consider that it may have really happened to a flesh and blood person, to Jesus.

This is one point where the Christian viewpoint radically differs from the Buddhist, Hindu or atheist viewpoints. The atheist would see the whole thing as impossible given his or her disbelief in a God-Reality. The Buddhist and Hindu, seeing the outer world as Maya or illusion, have no use for the saving of this illusory world. The Jew still waits, longingly, for the Messiah, still aware of the two worlds. It is the Christian who proclaims that the myth has become history, that the divine has burst into reality as a Personality and that this Personality is the great shaman who mediates between ego (or Soul in our diagram) and *both* worlds. It would do us well to remember that the early Christians experienced the Risen Christ as so real that they often confused their visions for outer reality. We moderns, who know a *little* more about perception, can speak of breakthrough of the nonphysical into the physical. This, as we have seen, happens all the time in shamanic healings and in psychosomatic illnesses in which emotion attacks the body. The Christian percipient sees a Personality as capable of breaking through in much the same way.

Who then is/was (how to ask the question?) this Jesus, whom Christians proclaim to be the Messiah? This is no easy question and we expect the answer to be flavored by one's point of view. Born in a stable, a carpenter, a learned and intelligent man, one who had a winning personality and great power; who could persuade others to follow him, a healer and miracle worker, a friend of whores and tax collectors, a man who cursed a fig tree and caused it to wither, a calmer of storms, a curser of hypocrites, an exorcist, and above all a great lover of men and women and children and life. This much the psychologists see and can allow into their framework (that is, the psychologists who have the point of view which we mentioned before. Those without this point of view can explain away what they need to as balderdash and as spontaneous remission, as fantasy and "myth" and delusional hocus-pocus.)

For the Christian percipient, however, another meaning, another explanation of Jesus' life, parallels and affects this first one. This is his divine origin, the Son of God, the Saver who protects the Christian from the forces of darkness, the Overcomer of death who shows the way to the Spirit.

It is this understanding of the Christian which is different from a purely psychological understanding and it is precisely this which troubles the non-Christian. Remember, though, Freud and Jung's statements; the nonexperiencer cannot believe the experience of another; the experiencer cannot convey a religious experience to one who has not had it. And so, the feud. But here it might be best to calm the inner storm and speak one to the other, Christian and non-Christian, Jew and non-Jew, Buddhist and non-Buddhist, theist and atheist. For there is really nothing to lose by listening, unless of course one is afraid of losing his viewpoint, in which case he probably needs to examine it anyway. This any good psychologist can tell you.

We are thus thrown back into the fray and two tasks become clear to us at once. There is the exploring and deepening of one's own point of view and simultaneously a sharing of points of view with others. It stands to reason that the more one explores his or her own point of view, the more he or she will have to share with another. The psychologist suggests that we get on now with the inner exploration.

In our diagram, we see that Christ plays a central role in the Christian's world view. This much is certainly no surprise. But what does it mean? How does this Messiah dead two thousand years (and arisen, in the Christian framework) affect the individual's life? Again two possible directions open for our searching: exploring what Christ was (is) about; and what the Christian does with what he is 'about.' My own preference is to further examine what we know about Christ first, in the hope that this will make the Christian's journey clearer.

There are many ways to look at Jesus (and many types and sociological situations from which to look at him). In the days of the relatively peaceful Roman Empire, for example, Christ might be expected to come to earth a second time to become Messiah and King of an earthly Kingdom, to bring his believers to power with him. Or in the Dark Ages, in a world of turmoil, panic, disease, and furious and uncontrollable change, Christ might be seen as the Saviour who rescues his people from this earthly vale of tears which, to those living in it, was no more than an unredeemable hell. Both these views are understandable. Yet a third position is that of an ongoing Incarnation (the attitude of many Christians in the early church), which takes both worlds into account. According to this view, there exist both a transcendent reality and a physical one to be dealt with; individuals have certain conceptions of what these two realities are and how they interact with each other (if for them both do exist); the Incarnation is a statement to the Christian of what these two realities are and how they can and do interact.

To the Christian, the Incarnation states the possibility of the divine or the transcendent meaningfully, really, and actually becoming physically alive in our world. Jesus is for the Christian, the Way, the Truth and the Life. In our terms, this means that for the Christian, Jesus joins the journey and even helps one pass through the narrow gate which for Jesus is the way, rather than the broad path. Psychologically, this might mean a coming to acceptance of one's individuality, and a laying claim to the responsibility of managing one's own path. At any rate, the Christian sees Jesus as his or her guide and protector as he or she moves toward, and through, the narrow gate.

Narrow gate? It's hard for left brain to sit quietly forever. What narrow gate? Why would one want to go through it anyway?

The response can only be "Please be patient, left brain, for we are presently out of your domain. What we are trying to do is to set up the framework so that you will know with whom you are interacting."

The narrow gate is after all an image, is right-brain language. Left-brain's question brings us to another aspect of the Christian's Jesus. We have remarked before that he is a healer and for Christians, the Messiah, and further, as the Incarnation, the physical manifestation of the Great Spirit or God. But with all this he is also a teacher and his teaching, as we might expect, brings no solace to the left brain, for his teaching is about his perception of reality and his method for dealing with reality, which isn't solely analytical.

Looking in the New Testament, we find that his teaching, to a great degree, is done through parables; he speaks in images which to the Christian relate the nature of the world. The Christian would go so far as to say that Jesus uses parables because he has to, since rational intellectual language cannot convey this reality, does not know this world. The Christian would further tell us that through these parables, the same reality is available today, as it was in New Testament times.

This much we remember is in line with Ornstein's work (1972) with Eastern traditional esoteric psychologies. One is led again to ask what's the difference then which tradition one uses? But the Christian claims that there *is* a difference and this necessitates our looking deeper into the Christian reality with which he or she relates.

The problem seems to be twofold. On the one hand, Jesus is the most materialistic of major religious leaders in that he proclaims the value of the body and its health and of the physical world, while on the other hand he sees great spiritual demonic forces with which the individual has to contend. And the kicker is that he claims to conquer evil so that one may turn to him when confronted with radical evil, the Evil One, who Jesus sees as a real and live Personality. Here we come close to the Christian's profession, and we can soon begin to look at how the Christian interacts with the world, given this profession.

Ironically, for many in our time, it is Jung and his followers who have reopened the door for religious and Christian experience. For until our first diagram was possible again (p. 105), our second diagram was cut off from society's view, because it was impossible, superstitious and fantastic.

One thing that Jung's brand of psychology shows us is the

(again) extreme importance of one's point of view. Fantasy, for instance, can be seen as wish fulfillment, or as a reality, in which one can find new solutions for one's problems. Myth can be understood as a story which is untrue, or as a story which shows one a different part of reality. Images are mere phantasms, or real figures, to be dealt with according to one's point of view. And this very point of view, to a great degree, determines one's path, one's journey; it determines what facts of reality will be considered. The Christian simply considers different facts than the Buddhist, than the atheist, than the materialist. For the psychologist to deal with the Christian, or anyone, it is necessary to consider that person's world view.

This brings us to the important questions of delusions and hallucinations. For certainly anyone who has visited a state hospital will have to admit that delusions and hallucinations do exist among the many Christs, Napoleons and miserable souls who live there. From the present perspective, this is not denied, but delusions and hallucinations are seen as the mistaking of inner experience for outer reality which prevents one from proceeding with one's outer life. In other words, the ego is not strong enough to decipher which world it is perceiving at any one time.

Now we see the danger in getting involved with the inner world and it is not only on the back wards that this danger exists. All around us, there are exploded minds stretched beyond their elasticity by drugs. There are burned and mangled bodies, compliments of Hitler, Stalin and others who confuse their inner darkness with whole races of people, and who then set out with missionary zeal and eager followers to accomplish their goals. There are also the interpersonal hatreds, and race hatreds, and sex hatreds, and class hatreds, which are based on similar delusions of individual, racial, sexual and class grandeur. As we look even closer, we see an awesome array of problems which may stem from a fear of facing ourselves and our inner world, which we consequently project on the outer world and other people. One with a materialistic stance, who

MASTERS OF THE HEART

posits no inner world, will have to let this darkness go outwardly or repress it or both.

The Christian, however, who understands these goings-on
sees the utter necessity for a Saviour, for Christ. The Evil
One, for the Christian, as for the modern doctor, is to be
combatted and overcome but the Christian will tell you that he
or she can do this only with Christ. In other words, the Evil
One has superhuman power which ego by itself cannot defeat.
The humility we spoke of earlier is essential here for one can
even be destroyed by the Evil One if he or she arrogantly or
unconsciously tackles this Greater Evil Power singlehandedly.

It will occur to the psychologist that this attitude can easily
slip one right into the onesidedness we are speaking of. For it
isn't a long step from here to making one's method the right
method for battling Evil, and one's definition of what (or who)
is evil the "true" definition, and then making oneself the "good
guy" whose mission is to eradicate this evil from the world.

The Christian will answer the psychologist that he has no
such luxury if he is open to the sayings of Jesus. For he is told
to see the log in his own eye before he sees the sliver in
another's, i.e., he must face his own darkness before he goes
after the darkness of his neighbor. And Jesus didn't feel a
special affinity to the good guys of his time, the Scribes and
Pharisees, calling them vile serpents and hypocrites. Ultimately, for the Christian, the Evil One has real, and much
more than personal, power which can capture him forever and
which he must constantly battle, never believing that he is
finally one of the good guys.

This 'forever' quality is something easily questioned and
brings us back to the reality of death, which don Juan sees as
so important. This question can be avoided no longer as it is
one of the cornerstones of the Christian framework. But it is a
very touchy issue, one which will need both left brain's and
right brain's cooperation. (In the end, all major questions seem
to need our whole mind, analysis and imagination. In this case,
where there is such disagreement, this is especially important

116

from the outset.) The Christian will speak of "life everlasting", of being "forever in Christ", of being united with Christ after death. The materialist will scarcely be able to hold back a chuckle at this "hopelessly meaningless wishing". Our logical mind ("left brain" as we are calling it) must step in here to clear the issue. It sees three possibilities: the materialist, the agnostic and the spiritual positions. The materialist, the agnostic and the spiritual positions. The materialist position states that we live in a cause-effect world of matter into which no supernatural meaning can possibly enter. The agnostic position states that one simply cannot know whether such super-material meaning is or is not real. The spiritual position has it that there does exist an experienceable, spiritual meaningful reality to which one can relate.

Logically, the materialistic position is the weakest of the three for the hardest proof in logic is of the non-existence of anything, presupposing as it does that one has been everywhere and knows everything about the world. The materialist (maybe unconsciously) is stating that he or she knows beyond a doubt that a spiritual reality does not exist. This is an impossible knowledge. The agnostic position fares better logically, for it at least admits its ignorance. It states what it doesn't know and proceeds from there. "Left brain" is much more comfortable here except that it wonders whence it will get its information for deduction if the stand is merely one of ignorance. About the third position, "left brain" is more tentative, for it is this position which offers the most information while at the same time offering most resistance to its scrutiny. It sees this as the potentially most dangerous and creative position where one can get lost in makyo if he or she doesn't submit to examination, or where one can report his or her experience and relate it creatively to one's establihed framework, see how it fits, and make necessary adjustments.

"Left brain" thus finds in favor of the methodology of the third position, the position which grows beyond agnosticism. It does not, however, make judgment on the *value* of the experience itself. The experience is given; our logical mind merely examines the given and by so doing gives us permission to explore the viability of the Christian experiences of life and death, and life after death.

We can now proceed to see what this experience might be. The problem "clear and simple" is this. The Christian story has it that Jesus, the man and Messiah, suffered a horrible and ignominious death and rose again from that death, conquering it forever. Well, then, why is there still death, this now conquered creature? This automatic question, which may be a formulation of positivistic thinking (why, why, why), may cloud the issue. We would do well again to remember the early Christians who marched confidently, and often joyfully, to their own deaths. For them death remained a certain reality but because of their new viewpoint, their new understanding of the world, death became a lesser reality in the face of their experience of the Risen Christ who, again according to their experience, opened them to a deeper Love which conquers death, a Love which lives around death, in spite of death, through death, and after death. In other words, they experienced a Love, a Life, greater than death.

But don Juan told us that death is one's best friend and this may help to make things clearer. What death does is to demonstrate to us strongly and emphatically our mortality, our relativity, our utter smallness. We speak here not only of physical death but also of psychological death, the death of who one is, of one's standpoint, in life. If death is to be our best friend, this is because it allows us the possibility of shedding our solipsism, our belief that we are the whole world, and stepping beyond it. This is no pleasure trip. One is then open to the terrible and beautiful world and, if not careful, subject to being utterly overpowered by this world. These aren't idle words, as Castaneda tells us in no uncertain terms. Again, for the materialist, this is the worst of all possible worlds, a veritable hell of delusion from which to recoil with great speed—if possible. I often wonder if our fear of the dangers of drug experience isn't to a great degree a projection of the fear that we will lose our materialistic standpoint if this drug experiencing doesn't stop. For aren't these drugtakers looking for an altered consciousness beyond our allowable material world?

This returns us to death, for the death of one's materialist standpoint is worse even than physical death because after it one is still there! For the Christian, as for the thinkers who see a weaving purpose in evolution, there may be meaning in all this. Drug experiencers are pointing (albeit unconsciously) to facts of reality which we normally ignore. The frequent "flashbacks" of some LSD users (i.e. which occur without another ingestion of the drug) suggest, for example, a reality from which these experiences come which LSD taps. The Christian has a framework (as do the shamans and medicine men) for allowing a relationship to this other world without the use of drugs. It is the fault of the modern religious institutions which have forgotten this that youths have been forced to turn to drugs to seek life and a meaning for life, to escape meaninglessness. In our diagram, Ego (or Soul) must give up its particular standpoint, letting that standpoint die, and this is often experienced as a hell as real and terrible as any afterlife hell. By letting the standpoint die, as we said before, one is opened to the terrible and beautiful world, and finds out quickly enough that he or she has met more than an equal. This is why don Juan, the shamans and all others who know this terrible world insist on the extreme importance of having a guide and protector. For the Christian, Jesus, as the embodiment of the Great Spirit, can be this guide and protector.

But we are in many ways talking around the death issue rather than confronting it. The Christian position (and hopefully we have not forgotten that there have been, and are, many, different "Christian positions") is that one must give up one's life to gain it. Concerning psychological death (the death of one's standpoint) this means giving up the certainty of one's life to be open to the Great Spirit within, allowing oneself to be dismembered and put back together by the Spirit so that he

119

or she may be a hole through which the Spirit may enter the world. The Christian experiences this Spirit as the Great Lover and feels himself or herself as truly lovable. There is, in other words, a symbolic (and very real) death of the individual followed by his or her experience of the Lover, who restores him or her and brings him or her to a new level of life. Concerning physical death, the Christian sees Christ, the physical embodiment of the Great Lover, as giving himself to death and sinking into the utter hell of it; and by so doing, conquering it for Love, so that Love could reach even beyond death and transform our afterlife. Thus the early Christians literally had nothing to fear as they met their deaths, for they experienced Love, and their relation to Love, as greater than death.

Still, one can't help exclaiming "Afterlife! It's built on straw. No one can know this!" In response, we should note that the word "afterlife" is based on an assumption that there exists something beyond material existence. As we have seen, no one can with absolute certainty prove that there is no other life than what one knows. It is more a question of experience. What then are the modern experiences? Two samples will be suggestive. Kalish and Reynolds conducted a study of individuals' experiences with others known to them to be dead. Of the 434 respondents divided approximately equally among Black, Japanese, Mexican and European origins, they found that 44 percent responded that they had had such an encounter in which they had been visited in person, at a seance or, most often, in a dream by the dead person. Raymond Moody, MD, has collected in *Life After Life*, more than 100 cases of "clinically dead" patients who have been resuscitated and who report having experienced a reality which *convinces them beyond a doubt* that there is life after death (See also Watson, 1974, Matson, 1975, Wheeler, 1976). One might at least wonder, if he or she assumes the inner and outer worlds as equally real, "where" that dead individual goes and what the next step of the journey may be like. Or the materialist might wonder why so many are susceptible to attaching meaning to these experiences.

At any rate, the (this particular) Christian viewpoint can be summarized generally as follows. The Christian experiences both the inner and outer worlds as real. At first, he or she develops an ego standpoint for viewing these worlds. Then, in the "Christian" experience, this ego standpoint dies and the individual may encounter, after much pain and fear, the Great Lover, who pieces the individual back together and restores him or her to the world with a new perspective and a new level of awareness. With physical death, the Christian continues along the Way, buoyed and protected by Christ, as he or she was in the earthly life.

But what practical implications does this have? What is the new level of awareness and what does one do with it? It is these practical implications which are most important for it is these which show others what this experience means. "Show us something which isn't ineffable," the materialist says, "something which we can sink our teeth into." This is a fair demand, but no easy task for that. And we cannot totally rely on the experience of the early Christians. We need something present, more immediately reachable. A return to psychology will be an aid here, as it has so often been on the present journey. This time, however, we will be examining a Christian psychology, seeing if it can be a viable means for an individual on his way.

The Christian psychologist as does the Jungian, but not the behaviorist, positivist, or materialist psychologist, sees himself or herself as mainly a mediator or shaman who attempts to put the individual seeking help in touch with the creative power of the Holy Spirit or the Self. The Christian psychologist further sees Christ as the best and truest way to the deepest experience of the Self, while the Jungian may not see it thus. I fall somewhere between these two positions, or with both of them, at this point in my own journey. A great deal depends on the particular individual, as we shall soon see.

Now imagine a person who would seek out a psychologist of

121

the Christian and/or Jungian variety (or psychological help, period). This person has come (for example) because he is overcome with fear and anxiety, is surrounded by the utter meaninglessness of his life and cannot continue living under such tension. How would the Christian psychologist deal with this person? (Remember that we are talking here of one with a framework similar to the one developed on this journey so far.)

First of all, he will see the person as a suffering individual who has lost his roots, and whose cure will grow out of himself as he sinks new roots. The psychologist will see himself as the mediator between the sufferer and his inner depths, and he will attempt to help the person establish the most creative relationship to these depths. As a Christian, the psychologist will (given the situation) offer the Christian framework as a way for establishing this creative relationship to the depths. Let's imagine that the particular individual is in extreme need of establishing such a relationship and see how the work might unfold. (The trouble that I'm having now expressing myself succinctly is to me the "precious" trouble, i.e., the trouble of people being so different from each other that each is his or her own special case. The present example will be just that, a look at a particular person and how to proceed with that person.)

Our sufferer is a man who has entered middle age and finds within himself a strange and frightening change. All of a sudden, successful though he is, he realizes that all that he has held dear and valuable and placed his love and energy in has suddenly lost its meaning. His dreams have become so powerful that he can't even shake them during the day, especially that horrible image of getting sucked down the drain of his swimming pool. What has happened, he wonders. He has always worked hard, and continues, when he is able, to work. But it's not so easy now, it's not natural. His wife and kids don't understand him. What they see is a fearsome grizzly lumbering about the house. He'd been a Catholic, always assumed its truth but never had to rely on it. Now, when he could use it, he finds instead a dry well. His anger knows no bounds. There is in him, he sees, a vicious hatred and some strange immense power which at any moment will overcome him. What has happened?

The Christian psychologist (as would many others) listens. And listens. He may pray to himself, "Jesus, Holy Spirit, let me be open to him, a channel of your will." Outwardly, he will empathize and try to help the man (let's call him Ralph) see that he isn't totally alone, that his experience isn't unusual for a man his age, that there is hope that this very experience will add a new dimension to his life. Together they will look at Ralph's dreams. He will be encouraged to keep a journal of his dreams, fantasies, moods and emotions and gradually Ralph will begin to see an inner world fully as real and powerful as the outer world, one which has been affecting him even though he wasn't aware of it. The psychologist will point out to him that the religions of the world weren't indulging in frivolous activity when they developed forms of ritual and prayer. This gives Ralph a new way of understanding the potential of his own religion, its symbols and rituals. Ralph comes to see that Jesus, too, was deadly serious about what *he* was about, that he embodies the Great Lover, and as such battles all which isn't creative for the individual. The psychologist shows Ralph that if he will try it, he can come into meaningful relationship with this creative source, who will support him in his ongoing battles after that; and Ralph will return to the fray, able to battle, having found a meaning in his life.

This imagining points to many things on which we should elaborate. First, such a brief account omits the blood and suffering of Ralph's journey, something which will be there all along the way, even after (perhaps especially after) his contact with Christ. Second, ritual and prayer are seen to be important. The psychologist himself prays for openness, so that he may be as creative as he is called to be in this situation. One reason that ritual is so important is that it gives the individual a tried channel for experiencing the divine, a reality so powerful that it needs channeling to become somewhat manageable. Ritual allows one to step into a world of images and myth, allows one to act out the myth bringing it to present reality. Ralph needs to experience a meaningful myth in his life and ritual offers him the possibility of finding it.

With ritual, we encounter again those suspicions of pre-modern superstitions. But viewed from another angle, this need not be the case. For scientific method is itself a ritual, one which in many cases must be strictly followed to obtain best (and often safe) results. Consider work with nuclear energy. Using one ritual, the scientists create conditions for beneficial societal use of the energy. Following another ritual, nuclear power may be unleashed in the most destructive, catastrophic ways. And with no ritual at all, there's no telling what kind of nuclear mess might surround us. For those whose inner world is as real and powerful to them as the outer world, ritual serves the same important function. It gives one a predictable channel for experiencing inner reality. As with the scientific method, the ritual chosen exposes one to inner reality in different ways, some rituals being predictably more dangerous than others. And for those with no ritual at all, one never knows whether the outcome will be a spiritual atom bomb or a spiritual power plant. This perhaps helps explain what happens to many drug users who are surprised by inner reality.

Ritual, both scientific and religious, is important for another reason. It gives the individual a contact with the ages, with other times and places. By so doing it tempers the individual, humbles him, shows him the debt he has to all that is beyond him for what he has become and for how he chooses to proceed. The psychologist will want to connect the individual with this creative source of collective wisdom. The sacraments, for example, and other rituals will thus become means for sacred play, for participation in the inner world as is the experimental method a means of creative play for scientists. One should not belittle this attitude of play, especially as one remembers that the individual's attitude is so important for what he or she discovers in the world.

But this sacred play may not prove satisfactory for Ralph, for he has tasted the inner world for himself, has experienced something of the bomb which, no matter how hard one tries, cannot be contained in the power plant developed by others; the craters and scars and miles of inner desolation cannot be forgotten on orders from some Dostoevskian Grand Inquisitor. With this, we reenter the psychological domain. For while the bomb has humbled Ralph, it also has forbidden his entrance to "the land of milk and honey". He may allow this as sufficient for others and as necessary for himself but, hard as he may try, ritual does not contain his experience.

The psychologist, the student of the psyche, of the individual, agrees with Ralph and encourages him to see the worth in his individual experience though it may deviate from ritual. But, acknowledging the inner reality, he sees that Ralph needs some formula, some method for dealing with this inner world much as the scientist needs a method for dealing with the outer world. The Christian psychologist will show Ralph that this inner formula or method is carried out through listening to the spontaneous activity of the inner world, through prayer and meditation. As we have noted before in many places, the individual's viewpoint will affect what he experiences. A Christian psychological framework will affect Ralph's inner experiences differently than, say, a Buddhist psychological framework.

In Ralph's case, with his Christian background (which obviously is an important factor), the Christian psychologist will offer a method in keeping with the Christian diagram proposed earlier (p. 109). The diagram will offer him a way for exploring his experience, testing it, working creatively with it as he battles the destructive elements and opens himself to the creative elements within. With this framework, he can listen to his dreams and begin to pray his individual prayer and meditation for he now has protection individually with Christ or the Holy Spirit as he had protection offered him ritually before.

Now that he can do this, what will Ralph's experience of the inner world be? As we never tire of saying, the method or formula will determine to a great degree what he experiences. In this case, the words "prayer" and "meditation" can have many different meanings depending on the goal of one's efforts. Ralph is searching for a meaning in life beyond himself, for he has understood clearly the insufficiency of his own meaning. Christian meditation can be offered him which opens him to the possibility of this greater meaning. He is encouraged to become quiet, to relax, to enter a state beyond his inner dialogue, but with a different purpose than Eastern meditation. For he is to let images arise and then *relate* to them and whenever, as he relates, the images become too difficult or threaten to overcome him, he is to call on an image of the Christ to protect him.

Protection from an image! Some may protest, as may Ralph, to which the psychologist can only answer, "Ralph, try it. You have nothing to lose anyway. It can be no worse than it is now." So if he will, Ralph begins his confrontation and perhaps (there's still no certainty) he will find to his amazement that it works, that images take life and that Christ protects him as he goes. This procedure is the same as Jung's active imagination, but "Christianized". It is not unlike the use of images by scientists to use and better understand the outer world. (Recall that Einstein let images dance before him and fall into place. Kekule, too, through a dream of six snakes eating each others' tails developed his model for the benzene ring in organic chemistry, which model has been very important for the further development of the field of organic chemistry.)

As Ralph uses active imagination, he finds that it can be an excruciatingly lonely experience and that it does not transform all his suffering meaningfully. The psychologist does two things for him now. He encourages him to attempt to reenter a ritual, to experience his deepest intimations of humanity and

126

reality in celebration with others. For Ralph must learn that suffering isn't the only avenue to growth. Joy and communion with other experiencers can offer a growth, or a way of letting go of oneself, which suffering alone cannot. This again is an experiential synthetic statement which cannot be decided logically; Ralph must try it to decide for himself.

Besides this possible joy (which, too, is not to be taken for the only way of growth), Ralph now needs to enter into conscious relationship with his protector. The psychologist shows him that he can begin this process by turning to Jesus' life and words, especially the parables, to see what Jesus was about. One problem Ralph may encounter will be his insistence on understanding the parables rationally. He is reminded that this is to force the parable into his understanding of the world rather than turning his understanding to a new possibility. This brings us back to the problem of one's framework. As Whorf tells us, language is both creative and limiting; it makes things possible but limits and excludes other possibilities. So, too, with one's framework. The psychologist is simply reminding Ralph of the limitations of his framework and his need to be open to new possibilities, to the beginnings of a new language or framework. Looking at the parables might be quite surprising, then. It may even be that their purpose is to surprise, to shake one up, to offer new possibilities of awareness and action.

Ralph thus turns to the New Testament in hopes of finding his relationship to Jesus and his teachings. The psychologist encourages him to react emotionally to the account, to let his soul stay where it wishes as he reads, to light where it will. He knows that it is for Ralph to find what is important for himself; only Ralph who feels the tender sore spots in himself which can be touched by his meeting. At first, it is all so familiar; he's heard it over and over and over through his years of education and Church attendance. Then he reads the account of the lost sheep. "What man among you with a hundred sheep" Jesus asks, "losing one would not leave the ninety-nine in the wilderness and go after the missing one till he found it? And when he found it, would he not joyfully take it on his shoulders, and then, when he got home, call together his friends and neighbors? 'Rejoice with me,' he would say. 'I have found my sheep that was lost.' In the same way, I tell you, there will be more rejoicing in heaven over one repentant sinner than over ninety-nine virtuous men who have no need for repentance" (Luke 15:4-7). Ralph's pulse hurries. But why? He's heard the story so many times before. First, it's the shoulders, the strength of the man who would carry the lost sheep that transforms the story around him. For Ralph knows the shivering fear of being lost, alone, away from the flock, defenseless. To think that his shepherd might rejoice at finding *him*! This stirs a crazy laugh deep within him and he reads with renewed interest. Almost immediately (Luke 15:11-32), he comes upon the parable of the prodigal, the ungrateful, son who takes his inheritance and squanders it away, and then returns to his father asking only to be hired by him as a laborer so that he may survive. But his father rejoices and has an incredible feast for him! The father does not stand in judgment but lovingly and joyfully welcomes him home. Ralph feels these arms opening for him, lost sheep and son, and sees the feast celebrated for *his* return. He has found Jesus now and can begin in relationship with him.

The Christian psychologist approaches other people with whom he works in a similar way. So much, however, depends on the individual's response, on where the person is emotionally and spiritually. Ralph is Ralph. This tautological statement is important for what it implies. Susan, for example, is not Ralph. Susan needs to be met as Susan not as a copy of Ralph. Ralph's work is not suited for her. Her emotional situation may be such that she doesn't need to hear this "mumbojumbo" now, that shoving this down her throat may be terribly destructive. She may be wired to a different power plant. All the psychologist can be for Susan or Ralph, or anyone, is the shaman, the hole through which creativity may come to him or her.

All of us obviously are on different journeys and we must respect each other's way. This is not to say that we are to deny our own way whether it be Christian psychologist, Buddhist anthropologist, Hindu truckdriver or whatever. Susan, or anyone working with him, has the right to know (or not to know) what the psychologist's way is and how that way goes for him, how he understands it, why he follows it.

This brings us to a very important point, although an obvious one. The psychologist, as is anyone else, is on his own journey, has his own confrontations, and has his own story to tell. His work as psychologist is part of this telling and he will best help those with whom he works by being that 'story' as honestly as he can. Freud and Jung demanded that all analysts first be analysed. In the same spirit, it could be said that the analyst or psychologist enters upon an ongoing analysis, a lifelong one, in which he sees that this constant looking is the awareness and experiencing of his journey, in the same way that he tries to help others become conscious of their journeys. The Christian makes no claim to final understanding of the Way, but rather makes a commitment to a framework which allows himself and others to be open to the constantly surprising depths of themselves and others. It won't be denied that there are other ways and it may turn out to be part of one's journey to explore these ways. But again (some will say unfortunately) one's framework will be important. The world is a dangerous place where one may easily be squashed like a bug. The psychologist, that student of persons, will need to know all he can about persons, their cultures, myths, dreams, depths, religions, and experiences. To be most helpful, he will have to be open to the facts of their lives and to the many possibilities that life will offer. This requires a humble attitude, an openness to surprise, and a commitment to a framework which makes these "red sixes of spades" visible.

Chapter 9 *Deeper Within*

One of those red sixes of spades may be about to appear.
For me, as for most anyone, this brings no comfort or good
tidings, especially in this dark tunnel. We were almost able to
forget the darkness for awhile, almost convinced that the
darkness was really light as we considered the psychologist's
and the Christian's roles. We had the answer and the darkness
need trouble us no more for it was conquered and we bathed
in the glorious holy light of victory. But something has
shifted. The darkness moves around itself, "darkness unto
darkness", and it closes in.

130

How easily I shifted back to we, picking up that shedded
skin hoping it would stick! The darkness now precurses the
greater Darkness. Images begin to bubble in the too-quietness. I
reach out to talk to you but you aren't there. And
the images. I would just talk and talk and talk to block
them—to anyone—even someone I hated. Anything, just to
stop them. The Darkness, dread fear, waiting to explode with
images of darkness, beasts, archetypes, angels, the Devil, call
them what you will. A snicker. Horrible gasping breath. Let
go, let go. No, if only someone to talk to, we could brush this

away.

I'm shaking. I am afraid. A cold wind tickles my face. It's all in your mind, some voice tells me. But so are you, Voice. So are you. The cold damp wind tickles my face . . . only in my mind. It isn't real. What! Yes, yes, Bultmann. It's just a formula, this myth stuff, a way of conveying truth, to the un-Enlightened. Whew! Yes, no, I'm not enlightened. Well, then, Barth. God dispensed with natural law for that time but then dispensed with the dispensation. But it doesn't work. What will stop God from dispensing with natural law again? And what of don Juan, Black Elk, the shamans? Other dispensations? Why was every other culture given the dispensation? Why does Campbell (1949) have to show these myths and images bubbling up everywhere in every culture? Why? Why did I have to find out about it?

Why?

Must quiet myself. Sit quietly, surrounded by the Quiet. The quiet almost a Shout-in-Absence, a bellow of some almost appearing monster. Remember my tools. Two realities. Inner and outer. Can deal with both. But use the language. Need the inner language in this tunnel. Two realities. And Christ. Way way too good a Way to come this way with me. Active imagination. Let go, let it happen. Christ will protect you. If only I could believe that.

Red six of spades. Surely your scientific curiosity is aroused. Discovery. This may be virgin soil. But the world is flat, you might fall off. There are monsters out there who will eat you.

I know now where I am. The labyrinth. Somewhere in this maze there is a Minotaur, who will kill me and eat me. I must find Theseus. Ariadne gave him the thread. But maybe he hasn't come yet, maybe not for another thousand years. I decide to retreat, to run out the way I entered.

What? I never noticed these two tunnels when I entered. Which way? And here again, which way out? Help! I am lost!

But no one hears me. Except the Minotaur.

Deeper Within

Shudders go through me, announcing Minotaur's approach. Will he come soon or will I first die of fear?

Rats run over my feet. One bites me. A bat zooms by my head. Is this the end of a journey, a horrible cold labyrinth, food for rats and Him?

My knees collapse under me. Only fear keeps me crawling. Fear and the little impossible hope. It can't end this way. I'll stumble onto the exit and get out. I'll escape.

I try to stand but now I cannot. The tunnel I have entered is smaller. I retrace my crawling. No good. No good. Daedelus outdid himself here.

Oh no! I have crawled into an area that prevents my turning around. I am almost stuck. At least Minotaur can't get me.

But there are snakes.

This fear paralyzes me for a moment. I listen. Nothing. Not a sound, no slithering, hissing, nothing.

I go on and as I proceed I am forced onto my belly. I crawl on my elbows and stomach, dragging my useless legs behind me. The skin on my elbow tears.

What's that? Was that a light? Is someone looking for me, a friend? Or is it Minotaur's cave, the dead end?

Oh I don't care. Anything to get me out of this choking tomb. Anything. I crawl into a large cavern. A sigh of relief goes through me as I realize that I can now stand. But still I cannot see. I am utterly exhausted, there's nowhere to go, and I collapse against the wall and fall asleep.

I dream that I am in a cavern and that I wake and get lost and must crawl on my belly like a snake until I enter a cavern and fall asleep and dream that I am in a cavern and that I wake and get lost and must crawl on my belly like a snake. . . .

I'm pinching myself. Am I awake now? Is this hell where I really am? And what can it matter? Is each waking a going deeper into sleep, into the pit, forever and ever and ever?

My last hope is gone—unless it is for the Minotaur that I hope, who will kill me and end this.

Or send me deeper and deeper into my dream.

My last hope is gone. All that is left is an immense perfect anger. I scream and bellow like the Minotaur, frustrated that no youths and virgins have been sent for my meal. If only that, I could live. . . .

But the empty horrid silence stretches eternal. I have been put in a labyrinth and become a Minotaur with no one to frighten. . . .

I rage and bellow and rush threateningly around the cavern often crashing into the wall. I scream and curse and blaspheme. All the hatred buried deep in me bursts forth in a cry of anguish and disgust . . . at the foolishness of it all, the utter damn foolishness of it all. Of course, drugs, alcohol, materialism—to forget for one stinking minute the hopelessness.

But what! The cavern is shaking, the whole earth shakes with the clomping of the monster. The *Real* Monster. I feel my skin. It is flesh, goosebumped but human. I am naked. My rage has called the Real Monster. He enters the cavern, formless Form, a walking Darkness, utterly visible to me in his Darkness. He is indescribably ugly. He has four heads and sees in all directions. The face that looks toward me grins horribly, a finger stuck between his front teeth hanging out.

"Human scum!" he shouts, four voices in one. "I devour all scum which enters my cavern."

"Oh, Jesus," I pray, my fear demanding the impossible. "Don't let him get me, Jesus."

A hand touches my shoulder from behind and I nearly faint. I turn to see a teenaged boy who has just lit a candle.

"Turn out that light!" screeches the Monster.

The boy walks toward him, holding the candle in front of him and the Monster retreats.

"What, you again! Get back! I cannot stand the light! He is mine! He came down here and he's mine! It is only just that I have him."

"You know that I am not only just," the boy answers softly. "The world would be yours if that were so." And louder. "Get

134

back! We must go on."

The Monster retreats, backwards, wary of the candle. As he backs out of the cavern he shouts over the boy to me, "Another time! I will catch you alone and then I'll have you." Then he is gone.

The youth returns to me and I recognize him now. He has the face of an old acquaintance, one whom I secretly hated for years, but behind the face is a deeper look which humbles me.

"You! But why would you risk yourself for me?"

"Because I love you."

"That's impossible. I hardly know you and . . . I never was too fond of you."

"That much is true. But it takes more than dislike to get rid of me."

"Like what?" I ask.

"Indifference. That would drive me away."

"I tried that but I couldn't do it. Something in you prevented that."

"And in you."

"I'm sorry."

"Come," he says touching my shoulder again, "let's leave this place."

"But how? It is a labyrinth."

"I know the way."

"Wait. One more thing before we go. How did you happen to be here?"

"I followed you."

"What?"

"Through the rats and tunnels, on my belly."

"Why didn't you say something then? Why wait until now?"

"Would you have listened to me then?"

"No, I guess I wouldn't have. I would have told you to get lost."

We both laugh at my unexpected joke. Then I say again, "I'm sorry."

"Don't be. You had to come this way. I wanted to come with you, to be here if you wanted me, but not to force myself on you."

"God, you really do love me."

"Do you know what you are saying?"

I suddenly recognize behind that face an old, old friend. That was the depth, my old dear friend waiting for me.

He climbs up the side of the cavern and the light of his candle shows the way, a steep opening. The rim of this tunnel is rough, natural, not like the labyrinth made by Daedelus, smooth but leading nowhere. I follow him.

"Be careful," he says offering his hand, "for it is a steep, steep climb."

I move cautiously, staying close. Soon, high above us, I see light, at the top of this steep underground mountain. After a long climb (I've slipped several times) we reach the top. My heart is pounding. How glad I am to see the sun again! I want to find the others, anxious to tell what has happened. I start walking and soon I notice that I am by myself. Quickly, I turn to see him, halfway back into the hole. He smiles at me.

"I have to go find another. Call me when you need me. I'll be there."

And then the strangest thing. Just before he disappears into the hole, he seems to transform, seems now to be a middleaged woman, but with that glow still burning through the face. I don't know. Maybe I just imagined it.

Chapter 10 *Above Ground*

And so, here I am, here we are, again. A slight tremble passes through my feet reminding me of the Minotaur. Perhaps it closes in on someone else now, perhaps in new form. Something in me automatically pulls for that person, whispers a prayer. "May you make it out. May you meet your friend."

But what can be said of all this? First (and again), we've come a particular way, down a particular path. There are so many other paths. In the religious realm, we've mentioned some of them, the Buddhist, Hindu, Judaic, Moslem, atheist

ways. Our way has led us to a Christian place, but this seems
to be in large part because we started out from a Christian
place. What if we stumble upon one of these other paths or if
someone seeking help is on one of these other ways? One thing
we can do is what John Dunne (1972) calls "passing over" by
allowing ourselves to sink into the truths of these other paths
and people and by permitting ourselves to feel the reality of
their truths. The next and equally important step is "coming
back" by bringing what we have learned back and seeing how
it fits in our framework, what issues it raises, what changes

139

can (and must) be made. For we have as much to learn from other persons, cultures, and religions as they have to learn from us.

In the scientific realm, we've used a Jungian framework. Again, a particular path. Other psychological paths include the Freudian, Adlerian, behavioral, transactional. It may be that one or another (or a combination) of these approaches will be the most creative and meaningful approach with a particular individual. In this case, it would be wrong to force a Jungian framework, or any other, on a person if that framework was less than creative.

Above all, on the journey, we are persons who happen to meet. (Whether it was "meant to be" or "by chance" doesn't matter here.) We can best meet if we come as we are and this is best accomplished by coming to know ourselves in all our suffering, neuroses, darkness and joy and by being open to the joy, darkness, suffering and neuroses of the other.

The journey we have taken suggests many answers to how we can do this. First, we need to be open to our own experience and we need a framework for understanding that experience. Next, we should be open to the experience of others, also checking the import of their experience for our framework. But as we have seen, being open to one's experience isn't all that easy; for there are things that we tend to see and things which are outside of our framework that we tend not to see, or to exclude as not important. Among these generally ignored facts or anomalies in our own culture are dreams, myths, extrasensory experiences, visions, religious experiences, the spiritual or unconscious deeper (and higher) world.

The scientific approach would have us investigate these experiences, test them out, and formulate theories which best explain them. The religious approach would have us experience them for themselves, as containers of reality and meaning. Together, both approaches can help us develop an inner and outer framework for these experiences.

Each journeyman will have his or her own way of exploring, or not, these experiences. If it is for the person not to explore, then that is how it is; one should never be forced. For those who would seek such experience, a number of suggestions can be made which are in line with the findings of the present journey.

First, in the individual sphere, it is usually best to turn at the outset to those spontaneous productions of the inner world, dreams and fantasies. If one is to establish a fruitful relationship with them, he or she will need to get to know them and the best way to begin is by recording them in a journal, for these anomalies, these red sixes of spades, quickly slip away if we do not note them at once. Here we find the first place where the individual needs to step outside of himself or herself. For shared dreams have a way of becoming more real. The sharer may be a spouse, friend, counselor, spiritual director, depending on what one needs. The Senoi Indians (Stewart, in Tart, 1968) give us one model for doing this, for they developed a method for sharing dreams at a family dream clinic every morning. As with dreams, many of the spontaneous fantasies should be shared and explored with a trusted person.

Another avenue of exploration is found through reading the creative fantasies of others. Using the present framework, one can understand the great artistic creations (one form of divine madness according to Plato) as attempts by these men and women to order their experiences of inner and outer reality. *The Gilgamesh Epic*, *The Odyssey*, *The Divine Comedy*, *The Tempest*, *Faust* are among these great attempts. Modern works which seek the same purpose include: T. S. Eliot's *Murder in the Cathedral*, *The Wasteland*, *The Cocktail Party*, and the *Four Quartets*; C. S. Lewis' *Chronicles of Narnia* (7 vol.) and *Space Trilogy*; Charles Williams' seven novels; J. R. R. Tolkien's *Lord of the Rings Trilogy*; David Lindsay's *Voyage to Arcturus*; Ursula LeGuin's *Earthsea Trilogy*; Evangeline Walton's modern novelistic rendering of Welsh mythology *The Mabinogion* (4 vol.). This list only scratches the surface (and there are other realms, e.g. the visual arts, music) but one who reads such fantasies with a framework similar to the one we have suggested will see the inner world bursting into flower, expressing a reality as real and as touching as outer reality.

The individual journeyer can also combine these two methods and produce his or her own personal experiences of the inner world in phantasy form. This production can have incredible effects on the imaginer who will want to approach the inner world with respect and care. It may be that writers such as Camus, Beckett and Sartre experience and express as they do (e.g. *The Stranger*, *The Fall*, *Waiting for Godot*, *Nausea*, *No Exit*) because they have not tapped the most creative aspects of the inner world, those aspects which lie beyond the Ego. Their imaginations can see the Void but not beyond it. The imagining journeyer who allows the possibility of the Beyond will find this Beyond weaving itself into his or her creations in a purposeful way.

Turning to religious literature, the journeyer will find that such literature often expresses approaches to inner reality similar to these imaginative efforts. Other journeyers from time immemorial have wrestled with, confronted, and imagined with inner reality. The journeyer will see losing battles as well as victories and may become confused as to what the proper approach should be. There are two suggestions I would make here. First, a psychological understanding which is open to these experiences will be extremely important. Jung's framework is the best one that I know. Second, a group of like-minded persons exploring this literature together can serve as a buoy, a marker, which reminds one where he or she is, of the relativity of his or her position. One approach (see e.g. Wink, 1973; Kelsey, 1976) is to examine Scripture with the purpose of including oneself in it. An example would be to take the birthright story of Jacob and Esau and to ask members of the group questions such as the following:

1) What part of you is like the blind Isaac in the story?
2) Who is the Esau in you who goes out to prepare the

142

meal?

3) What part of you is like Rebecca who would trick the rightful heir out of his inheritance, his birthright?

4) Who is the Jacob in you who will go along with such trickery?

5) Why does the trickster become Israel?

And so on. Working in such a group gives one a surprising number of insights and allows one to explore those parts of oneself which are stirred by the story.

Still another approach is through ritual. For me, this is the complementary opposite of exploring one's individuality in dreams and fantasies; it is as the wave of light is to the particle of light in physics. To experience one's fullness, the wave of one's life as well as the particle, requires a living connection to the history of one's group. Ritual can provide this connection by allowing one to participate in, to play in, the tribal connection with the Unknown. And as noted before, different rituals will prepare different connections. In searching for one's roots, one will want to go as deeply as possible into the ritual of his or her own tribe. As one approaches one's own roots, he or she will enter into a living relationship with the Source of the ritual. (See, e.g., Sanford, 1972.)

Next, Dunne's "passing over". One's particular journey may require him or her to explore other frameworks, rituals, belief systems. If one has gone to the roots of his or her own system, he or she will be better able to examine another system in its richness. But there is also the "coming back" when the person applies what has been learned to his or her root or "radical" self.

A basic problem that a person must wrestle with in "passing over" is whether or not to come back at all, i.e., whether to give up one's viewpoint, one's ego relation to reality. The problem is particularly clear when two viewpoints as radically different as those of Eastern and Western thought meet each other. In searching for our Western roots, we have seen that the ultimate goals of these two systems are radically different.

In the East, the goal is to merge with the Cosmic Mind, to give up one's ego once and for all, to transcend the opposites of the world in reaching for nirvana, satori, samadhi. The Western thought of modern science and ancient religion, on the other hand, generally sees the individual's development and attitude along the way as most important. While a person's ego standpoint may need to die, the ego must develop a new relationship to reality rather than ultimately passing out of existence. Indeed, with no ego, quantum mechanics becomes impossible, for the observer who views the world will have dissolved and there will be no experiment.

But the Eastern and Western "systems" announce again the feud which needs to be seen as clearly as possible, for the feud itself makes ongoing, important demands on all of us. First, it demands that we be careful, that we consider all sides of an issue and of our standpoint. If we don't, if we avoid the feud, we will become sloppy, assuming as certainties things which are uncertain. Second, the feud demands radical commitment. Knowing as we do the importance of one's point of view for what one sees, anything less than commitment will cause one to be blown about in the wind, never settling, never becoming fully what one can be. Third, the feud demands self-knowledge for only by knowing where one stands can he or she continue the feud.

It may be then that the feud is a motivator which forces each person and each aspect of a person to examine himself and itself more deeply. The right brain must find its own truth if it is to become more acceptable to itself and to the left brain, and part of this truth can only be gained through an openness to what left brain knows about it.

So it is with the materialist and spiritualist, Christian and Buddhist, scientist and religious person.

The ongoing feud, within and without. No permanent peace but moments when "corpus callosum" brings the two together, when the stretching opposites give way to transformation and a new truth, which includes and transcends both, emerges . . . before the feud begins again.

Now, I end where we began, at the beginning. But at the end, there is that thorn, the particular way and commitment to that way. For with the openness, there is a framework and a commitment. Here, now, for me, to psychology and to Christianity, and the two together, particles and waves of the same light. We must make our statements so that we can know each other, our relative statements of our paths, choices and experiences, each of which is a challenge, a continuation of the feud, by those committed to different truths.

Or if the feud should change its mood, we can stop for a moment, each on his or her particular path, each at a beginning, and listen to another imaginer before we go our own ways.

"For most of us, there is only the unattended
Moment, the moment in and out of time
The distraction fit, lost in a shaft of sunlight,
The wild thyme unseen, or the winter lightning
Or the waterfall, or music heard so deeply
That it is not heard at all, but you are the music
While the music lasts. These are only hints and guesses,
Hints followed by guesses; and the rest
Is prayer, observance, discipline, thought and action.
The hint half guessed, the gift half understood, is
Incarnation.
Here the impossible union
Of spheres of existence is actual,
Here the past and future
Are conquered and reconciled,
Where action were otherwise movement
Of that which is only moved
And has in it no source of movement —
Driven by daemonic, chthonic
Powers. And right action is freedom
From past and future also.
For most of us, this is the aim
Never here to be realised;
Who are only undefeated

MASTERS OF THE HEART

Because we have gone on trying;
We, content at the last
If our temporal reversion nourish
(Not too far from the yew-tree)
The life of significant soil."
        (T. S. Eliot "The Dry Salvages" in *Four Quartets*)

Bibliography

Assaglioli, R. *Psychosynthesis*. New York: The Viking Press, 1971.

Barber, T. X. *Hypnosis: A Scientific Approach*. New York: Van Nostrand Rheinhold, 1969.

Barber, T. X., J. P. Chaves & N. P. Spanos. *Hypnosis, Imagination, and Human Potentiality*. New York: Pergamon, 1974.

Barnett, L. *The Universe and Dr. Einstein*. New York: Bantam, 1968.

Bergson, H. *The Two Sources of Morality and Religion*. New York: Henry Holt and Co., 1935.

Boyd, D. *Rolling Thunder*. New York: Dell, 1974.

Bruner, J. & L. Postman. "On the Perception of Incongruity: A Paradigm." *Journal of personality*. 1949, *18*, 206-223.

Campbell, J. *The Hero with a Thousand Faces*. New York: Meridan, 1956.

Carlson, R. (ed.) *The Frontiers of Science and Medicine*. Henry Regnery, Chicago, 1976.

Castaneda, C. *The Teachings of Don Juan: A Yaqui Way of Knowledge*. Berkeley: U. Cal. Press, 1968.

——*A Separate Reality*. New York: Simon and Schuster, 1971.

——*Journey to Ixtlan*. New York: Simon and Schuster, 1972.

——*Tales of Power*. New York: Simon and Schuster, 1974.

Deikman, A. "Deautomatization and the Mystic Experience." in C. Tart (ed.) *Altered States of Consciousness*. New York: John Wiley and Sons, 1969.

——"The Meaning of Everything." in R. Ornstein. *The Nature of Human Consciousness*. San Francisco: W. H. Freeman, 1973.

Dessauer, F. "Galileo and Newton: The Turning Point in Western Thought." in *Papers from the Eranos Yearbooks*. J. Campbell (ed.) Vol. 1, New York: Pantheon, 1954, 288-321.

Dunne, J. *The Way of All the Earth: Experiments in Truth and Religion*. New York: The MacMillan Co., 1972.

Einstein, A. *Ideas and Opinions*. New York: Crown, 1954.

Bibliography

Eliade, M. *Shamanism: Archaic Techniques of Ecstasy.* Princeton: Princeton U. Press, 1964.

Eliot, T. *The Complete Poems and Plays, 1909-1950.* New York: Harcourt, Brace and World, 1962.

Ferguson, M. "Karl Pribram's Changing Reality." in *Human Behavior,* May, 1978, pp. 28-31.

Fire, J. (Lame Deer) and J. Erdoes. *Lame Deer: Seeker of Visions.* New York: on and Schuster, Simon and Schuster, 1972.

Frank, J. *Persuasion and Healing.* New York: Schocken Books, 1963.

Freud, S. *The Future of an Illusion.* New York: Doubleday, 1964.

Greeley, A. *The Sociology of the Paranormal.* Hollywood, CA: Sage, 1975.

Greeley, A. & W. McGready. "Are We a Nation of Mystics?" in New York Times Magazine. January 26, 1975.

Heisenberg, W. *Physics and Philosophy.* New York: Harper and Row, 1958.

Huxley, A. *The Doors of Perception.* New York: Harper and Row, 1954.

Jaffe, A. *The Myth of Meaning.* New York: Putnam's and Sons, 1970.

James, W. *The Varieties of Religious Experience.* New York: Collier Books, 1961.

Johnston, W. *The Still Point.* New York: Harper and Row, 1970.

Jung, C. *Psychological Types.* Vol. 6. Collected Works. Princeton: Princeton U. Press, 1971.

——*Archetypes and the Collective Unconscious* Vol. 9i. Princeton: Princeton U. Press, 1968.

——*Memories, Dreams, Reflections.* New York: Pantheon, 1963.

——*Modern Man in Search of a Soul.* New York: Harcourt, Brace and World, 1933.

——*Answer to Job.* Cleveland: World Publishing Co., 1960.

——*Psychology and Religion.* New Haven: Yale U. Press, 1938.

——*Analytical Psychology: Its Theory and Practice.* New York: Vintage Books, 1968.

Kelly, G. *A Theory of Personality.* W. W. Norton and Co., New York, 1955.

Kelsey, M. *Dreams: The Dark Speech of the Spirit.* New York: Doubleday, 1968.

——*Encounter with God.* Minneapolis: Bethany Fellowship, 1972.

——*Healing and Christianity.* New York: Harper and Row, 1973.

——*Myth, History and Faith.* New York: Paulist Press, 1974.

149

——*The Other Side of Silence. A Guide to Christian Meditation.* New York: Paulist Press, 1976.

——*The Christian and the Supernatural.* Minneapolis: Bethany, 1976.

——"The Art of Christian Love" (pamphlet) Pecos, N.M.: Dove Publications, 1974.

Kuhn, T. *The Structure of Scientific Revolutions.* Chicago: U. of Chicago Press, 1970.

Matson, A. *Afterlife.* New York: Harper and Row, 1977.

McGlashan, A. *Gravity and Levity.* Boston: Houghton-Mifflin, 1976.

Moody, R. *Life after Life.* Covington, GA: Mockingbird Books, 1975.

Leshan, L. *The Medium, The Mystic and the Physicist.* New York: The Viking Press, 1973.

——*Alternate Realities.* New York: Evans, 1976.

Murphy, G. *Human Potentialities.* New York: The Viking Press, 1975.

Neihardt, J. *Black Elk Speaks.* Lincoln, Neb.: U. of Nebraska, 1961.

Newcomb, F. *Hosteen Klah: Navaho Medicine Man and Sand Painter.* Norman, Okla.: U. of Oklahoma Press, 1964.

Oppenheimer, J. "Analogy in Science" *The American Psychologist. 11*, 1956, 127-135.

Ornstein, R. *The Psychology of Consciousness.* San Francisco: W. H. Freeman, 1972.

——(ed.) *The Nature of Human Consciousness. A Book of Readings.* San Francisco: W. H. Freeman, 1973.

Panati, C. *Supersenses.* New York: Quadrangle Press, 1974.

Pearce, J. *The Crack in the Cosmic Egg.* New York: Julian Press, 1971.

——*Exploring the Crack in the Cosmic Egg.* New York: Julian Press, 1974.

Perrin, N. *Rediscovering the Teachings of Jesus.* New York: Harper and Row, 1967.

Sanford, J. *The Kingdom Within.* Philadelphia: Lippincott, 1970.

Skinner, B. *Beyond Freedom and Dignity.* New York: Alfred A. Knopf, 1971.

Smith, A. *Powers of Mind.* New York: Ballantine, 1975.

Stewart, K. "Dream Theory in Malaya." In C. Tart (ed.) *Altered States of Consciousness.* New York: John Wiley and Sons, 1969, 161-170.

Tart, C. (ed.) *Altered States of Consciousness.* New York: John Wiley and Sons, 1969.

Teilhard de Chardin, P. *The Phenomenon of Man.* New York: Harper and Brothers, 1959.

Toben, B. with J. Sarfatti & F. Wolf. *Space-Time and Beyond.* New York: E. P. Dutton and Co., 1975.

Bibliography

Von Franz, M. & J. Hillman. *Jung's Typology*. New York: Spring Publications, 1971.

Watts, A. *The Joyous Cosmology*. New York: Pantheon Books, 1962.

Weil, A. *The Natural Mind*. Boston: Houghton-Mifflin, 1973.

Watson, L. *The Romeo Error. A Meditation on Life after Death*. New York: Dell, 1974.

Wheeler, D. *Journey to the Other Side*. New York: Grosset and Dunlap, 1976.

Wiesel, E. *Souls on Fire. Portraits and Legends of Hasidic Masters*. New York: Random House, 1972.

Whorf, B. *Language, Thought and Reality*. (ed. J. Carroll) Cambridge, MA: The MIT Press, 1956.

Wink, W. *The Bible in Human Transformation: Toward a New Paradigm for Biblical Study*. Philadelphia: Fortress Press, 1973.